LOSING IT.

the semi-scandalous story of an ex-virgin

a candid memoir by
danielle sepulveres

BRYCE CULLEN PUBLISHING

**BRYCE
CULLEN
PUBLISHING**

PO Box 731
Alpine, NJ 07620
brycecullen.com

ISBN 978-1-935752-12-7

Library of Congress Control Number: 2011943060

Printed in the United States of America

10 9 8 7 6 5 4 3 2 1

To Jen Stern, thank you for being my friend,
my biggest supporter, and my "favorite."
And to Marie Rose Antinoro Sepulveres,
known as Mary to most but as Grandma to me.
Thank you for believing that I could do anything.
I love you and miss you every single day.

contents

preface

*T*his book has been a labor of love. And disappointment. And basically every other sentiment a person can experience on the journey to achieve a very elusive and difficult goal. The bulk of it was written several years ago—as it all took place. Unfortunately, it has been sitting on a shelf collecting dust—until now. As I went through the manuscript to edit and look at it all through the eyes of someone with some distance and perspective, I was struck by the raw emotion behind my story. It almost felt as if I were reading about a complete stranger, compared to the place I find myself now. And I realized exactly why there are so many books written and films made about first love. Everyone in the world experiences it at one time or another, nothing else compares to it, and it kicks the shit out of you. And that is why I stopped myself from engaging in any heavy editing. This book is not about looking back on those experiences with a more mature, practical mind. It is about what happened, how it happened, how it made me feel—irrational or not—and the fact that I know it is important to share the dark parts as well as the inspirational. To do anything less would cheapen it. But I have changed names (except my own) and a few locations to protect the innocent, as well as the not-so-innocent.

Quite a few people would tell you that I have been known to be a kissing bandit, but I have only been able to say *I love you* to two men in my romantic life. The first time was an error in judgment. Overall, my relationship with #1 was undoubtedly the best and worst thing I ever experienced. Best because I can now spot a manipulative, selfish liar from eight miles away, and worst, well… you will see the worst in the forthcoming pages. All this heartache from #1 did prepare me for #2, but here is where I will stop myself from gushing about him, partly because I respect his privacy, but mostly because I will need material for my sequel. But this book is not just about first love; it is also about the very real and current issue of cervical cancer. In the United States, 11,000* women are diagnosed with cervical cancer every year, and about 4,000* women die from it. In developing countries, the deaths are estimated at 253,500*, all because adequate gynecological care is not available. This is a preventable cancer! Preventable with regular, yearly Pap test screenings, and yet, even in the United States, 11 percent* of women fail to make the effort to visit the gynecologist once a year for these screenings. I did not write this book as a cancer survivor, but as a cancer preventer. It is our responsibility to take care of our bodies to the best of our ability; early detection and early screening saves lives.

So, if you have ever been in love…. Had a health scare…. Lost your way in life…. Had absolutely no idea what you were doing…. Woke up and found it really hard to get out of bed one day (or many days)…. Then congratulations—you are officially a human being. And you are going to love my book.

Thanks for reading,
Danielle xoxo

*Statistics courtesy of National Cervical Cancer Coalition (NCCC)

prologue

TO DO IT OR NOT TO DO IT:
THAT IS THE QUESTION

*"It is one of the superstitions of the human mind to have
imagined that virginity could be a virtue."* —Voltaire

have no idea how other people go about making decisions regarding their virginity. How long to hold on to it, who to lose it
to, or if they even care about when and where it happens. I can
remember an episode of *Beverly Hills, 90210* (the original one—
not the skanked-out anorexic version on the air these days) from
when I was growing up that depicted main characters Brenda and
Dylan deciding to have sex on prom night. It was all so romantic
and perfect…until a few episodes later when Brenda was peeing
on a stick and dramatically telling Dylan she just was not ready to
be sexually active. And in school, health class began in the fourth
grade. So from age nine forward, the AIDS epidemic, teen preg-

nancy, and gonorrhea were paraded before our impressionable young minds. I seriously think that health class in my middle school was designed to scare the sex drive right out of you. Our textbooks depicted graphic images of people diagnosed with herpes, which was enough to put me off French kissing for a couple years. And even if you had a strong will (or major horniness) to dismiss the STD statistics, there was always *The Miracle of Birth* video in high school, which should be renamed *The Video That Will Make You NEVER Want Children—EVER*. The image of that video has been tattooed on my brain for more than a decade: a very hairy vagina expanding to a size that I swear God never intended, a slimy, snot-covered creature appearing, and then a huge, jellyfish-looking sack of blood sliding out. You really cannot get better birth control than that. I don't care if Yaz controls PMS and mood swings. It just does not compare.

It really was not just health class that made me wait so long to lose my virginity. I feel that there needs to be some level of comfort with your own body and the fact that someone else is going to see it in its entirety. I was definitely *not* comfortable with my body for most of high school, but when I finally *got* comfortable, there was no guy whom I liked enough to even take my top off for, never mind get totally naked.

For years I watched girlfriends of mine "know" when it was the right time. One lost it on a school trip to Scotland our junior year; another did it with a close guy friend because they were both curious. A few weeks later they were no longer friends. My best friend lost hers in college with her first serious boyfriend, and one of my college roommates lost hers to a guy who, unbeknownst to her, was accepting the V-card all over campus. And yet I still hung out on the sidelines. There were guys. There were *plenty* of guys.

But there was only one real possibility back then, who eventually fell out of the running due to some unfortunate circumstances, which will be discussed in Chapter 4.

I suppose I attribute a lot of different things to why I waited until I was in my early twenties: my own paranoia that grew out of paying too much attention in middle and high school health class, my idiotic decision to take Biology of Human Sexuality in college, my mother's insistence when I liked a guy to "just be friends, not sleep with him," and ultimately my belief that I would have a gut instinct telling me when I had met the right guy. Looking back, it is no wonder that I ended up in therapy.

"Hey, Dad, what does Immaculate Conception mean?" I was staring out the car window at a church we were passing. All the other churches I knew were named after a saint.

My dad coughed and then cleared his throat. "Uh…Immaculate Conception?" he coughed again. "It means that…well it's part of the, um, Virgin Mary story…it has to do with…uh—"

"Oh, Bible stuff?" I interrupted, bored already.

"Yes! Yes, Bible stuff." He still sounded uneasy and I did not understand why but decided I needed to change the subject. Being a Cashew (half Jewish and half Catholic), I had been able to opt out of attending CCD or Hebrew school, unlike most of my other friends. Anything Bible-related was really foreign to me.

Then there was the movie *Adventures in Babysitting*, a favorite for any female growing up in the eighties. Elisabeth Shue's character discovers her boyfriend cheating on her and, to justify himself, he makes a flippant comment about how her legs are locked together at the knee. At this point I questioned each of my parents as to what Bradley Whitford's character meant, but I was shushed and told to be quiet and just watch the rest of the movie.

But my favorite moment where my parents are concerned in relation to sexual activity was *The Talk* I was privy to the week before I left for college. The three of us were about to embark upon our umpteenth trip to Bed Bath & Beyond for more egg crates or God knows what else, when my mother decided she would remain home.

"I think I'll just stay here, the two of you go," she said, looking at my father with a weird expression and speaking far too loudly. Then she hugged me and whispered in my ear, "Your father wants to talk to you, just you and him." She let go of me and I stumbled back as she hurried back into the house.

The ride to the store was uneventful, as was the actual shopping while we discussed details of my upcoming move into the dorms at the University of Delaware. But the ride home took a turn for the awkward when my father grew silent and I could sense we were about to have an uncomfortable father-daughter moment.

"So uh," he cleared his throat, "uh I just want to tell you that you need to be careful when you go to college." He shifted in the driver's seat, clearly ill at ease.

A little confused at first, I responded thinking he was referring to partying and underage drinking. "Don't worry, dad, I know not to drink too much and never to put a drink down, walk away, and pick it back up again and—"

"No, no, I'm not talking about that," he interrupted, and then paused.

I sat there. *Uh-oh. I know where this is going.*

We sat there quietly, just the sounds of Cousin Brucie on the radio breaking the silence. My father cleared his throat again for his second attempt. "I just think you should know…." Another long pause ensued. Then it all came out in a rush. "AIDS will kill you and herpes is forever!" He relaxed back in the seat, visibly relieved to get the words out.

More than a little bit in shock, I quickly replied, "I know."

"Okay."

"Okay."

And again we rode in silence, he satisfied that he had done his part to keep me chaste, and I completely mortified.

A long time ago I did imagine that I would be a virgin until I got married, and I wonder if there are any girls who still believe in that scenario. I can actually pinpoint one specific instance when virginity first appeared on my radar as a hot topic.

The night ingrained in my memory was a sleepover with my friend Katie at the age of eleven. We had been friends since we were in diapers, always strikingly opposite in everything. I was tall; she was short. She was olive skinned with dark hair and dark eyes; I was fairer with light blue eyes and hair that had just turned from blonde to brown a few years earlier. Constantly the scaredy-cat, I was somewhat in awe of her bolder attitude when it came to most things—most things being the opposite sex.

"How old do you want to be when you 'do it?'" Katie looked at me curiously. I blanched at the question. My face reddened and I looked at her helplessly, fidgeting in my sleeping bag. I had never considered being a certain age when I finally *did it*; it would just happen when I was married…wouldn't it? "I want to be six-teen!" Katie declared emphatically. "We'll fall in love and have sex at sixteen, get engaged at eighteen, and married by nineteen." I gaped at her. She sounded so sure of herself—so confident—yet I still did not even know when I was going to wrap my head around the whole prospect of just tongue kissing. "So come on, Dani, what about you? When do you think you're going to lose your virginity?"

I giggled, wishing she would change the subject. Were we even old enough to talk about this stuff? "I don't know?" I offered, still blushing and grateful for the darkness of the basement to hide my face. "Whenever I get married, so maybe when I'm like twenty-four or twenty-five, I guess?"

"No!" she sounded horrified, and I scrunched further down in my sleeping bag as if I could hide from her disapproval. "You can't wait that long! That's just crazy! Nobody waits that long anymore, plus you'll probably be married long before that, don't you think?"

"Maybe," I said, unconvinced. In truth, I thought twenty-four was really young to get married, never mind nineteen. But my opinion was not the norm for a child of the eighties.

"But come on,"· she persisted, "what if you absolutely just are crazy in love with someone when we get to high school?"

I laughed; she was not going to let it drop. "Okay," I conceded, "if I am 'crazy in love' in high school then I will probably do it when I'm eighteen." I was lying through my teeth but hoping she would move on to another topic.

"Eighteen is okay," I could practically hear her nodding her head approvingly. "I want to have a bunch of boyfriends," she yawned sleepily. "All tall and really hot."

I lay there quietly, waiting for her to fall asleep, staring into the darkness of the basement. I wondered what would happen when we attended high school in a few years. Would Katie get her dream at age sixteen? Would she remember, when we were eighteen, what I had said? I rolled onto my side and closed my eyes. Eighteen was too young, I decided. Waiting for marriage was just the right thing for me, even if Katie denounced it.

Katie made it to her goal about three years early. Only two years after that sleepover she went "all the way" with her boyfriend, James. They were both thirteen. I was in shock, mostly because it did not seem to faze her even the slightest bit, as if it were perfectly natural. Then, following in the footsteps of Brenda Walsh, Katie had a panic attack and had to pee on a stick a few weeks later. Ironically, I ended up being the one counting out fifteen dollars and eighty-six cents for her store-brand maternity test. It was negative. And so on.

one

HEY...I'M PRACTICALLY A VIRGIN

"A woman is like a teabag—you can't tell how strong she is until you put her in hot water." —Eleanor Roosevelt

"You're single...but you're not available." The statement that my therapist uttered just moments earlier stuck in my head. I mouthed the words as I drove back to work. *Single. Not available.* It really was a nice turn of phrase. If only it were not indicative of the mess infiltrating my entire existence.

I had sat in Dr. Olsen's rocking chair, nervously folding and unfolding my hands. "So how have you been?" She peered at me expectantly through her round, pink glasses. All our sessions began this way, as if she already knew about the guilt-ridden confession I had stored away and she was giving me permission to reveal it.

"I'm good! I'm good…. I've been looking at apartments, just

haven't found the right one yet. Work, well…work is work," I coughed nervously, "and the beach house is great, as usual. The girls are great; we're having a great summer." *Jesus, could I use the word* great *one more time?* "Everything is…great," I finished weakly.

Dr. Olsen sat with her pen poised, her expression unchanged. "Are you dating anyone? Or have you met someone whom you would consider seeing socially or romantically?"

"Um, no." *Fuck.* I was starting to feel the way I do at weddings when long-distance relatives loudly ask why I did not bring a date and then start announcing to everyone within a hundred yards what a shame it is that I had arrived sans boyfriend.

"Have you had any more contact with your ex-boyfriend?"

There it was: the question I dreaded and yet hoped she would ask. After all, when you are lying to your family and friends about the fact that you are still seeing (i.e., sleeping with) your ex-boyfriend, there has to be someone whom you can tell—even if you do have to pay them.

"Yes, I saw Matt a few days ago. He called me and wanted to see me, so I drove to his house and we…talked." *Holy shit.* I felt my face turning red. I do not know if it was because Dr. Olsen had such a mom vibe to her, but sometimes when we talked about sex, I felt myself get nervous, as if she were going to lecture me. She never did, but I always had an initial discomfort when we hit on that particular topic.

"What did you talk about?"

Oh God. What did we talk about? We talked about how he could not stop thinking about me all through his business meeting and had to see me naked. We talked about how hard he got after he called me—so hard that he could barely walk to the door and let me in when I arrived. He said, "Oh baby." I said, "Mmmm, don't stop," and the conversation ended with a simultaneous groan, scream, and sigh.

"Well he told me how much he wanted me," I hedged, "and then we had sex. He said that he had been thinking about me nonstop and that he can't control himself around me. He said he wants to have me all the time."

"*Have* you or *be* with you?" Dr. Olsen was not one to play the semantics game. She made a few notes while I tried to think of a good answer. "You've said before that he can't deal with anything that might actually be an issue, that he runs anytime things get difficult."

"That's true, he does," I admitted cautiously. *But I still somehow love him, I thought despairingly. As screwed up as he is, he makes me feel things that nobody else has ever made me feel, and for some reason, I just cannot let go of it. I am one hundred percent addicted to him and how he makes me feel. Why don't I say this out loud? Because somewhere inside, I still know that he is wrong for me.* Humans as a race are largely unhealthy creatures, and sometimes we just cannot help ourselves. So I went to a shrink hoping she would help me. Even if I were too ashamed to admit certain truths, my hope was that she would have some sort of psychic ability to see right through the bullshit and fix me—in fifty-minute increments.

"How did it make you feel to see him?" She gazed at me with eyes like saucers. I waited for her to blink. She didn't.

"I don't know…good…bad…shitty. I felt sick on my way over because I knew I shouldn't go. I felt good when I was there with him, touching him and um talking—we did a *lot* of talking—and then shitty on my way home because I felt weak."

"Why did you feel weak?"

"Because all I think about is him, and when he calls I can't seem to stop myself from going to see him." I felt tears start to burn the inside of my eyelids. I really needed to stop crying over him. Until Matt came along I had not shed tears over a guy since the age of eleven. I took a breath and looked out the window to gather my thoughts. I felt a pain in my chest—the sharp pain that always arose when I really examined my situation with Matt. Was it worth it? An hour or two of being with him just to feel awful for days on end? Why did I keep subjecting myself to it? I looked up at Dr. Olsen. She smiled patiently.

"You're single…but you're not available," she said matter-of-factly.

"I'm what?" It seemed my diagnosis was a human oxymoron, emphasis on the *moron*.

"Technically you're not in a relationship, but you're not letting yourself be available for the possibility of a new one. Until you can completely remove yourself from this man's emotional grasp, you won't be able to fully engage yourself in any sort of new romantic relationship. You're probably ignoring any new possibility because you're holding onto the remnants of what you once had, compounded by the fact that this man will not step back of his own accord. You are going to have to be the one to make that final break."

"I meet new guys…sometimes," I offered faintly.

She smiled again. She knew that I knew that she was right. That mountain of hurt surged up again in my chest. And then my fifty-minute hour was up.

Back at work, I could not get the session out of my head. I fervently wished that I had a job inputting data into a computer for eight hours instead of dealing with obnoxious clients and insecure candidates. I was far too distracted to coddle each interviewee and put on my tough negotiator act for the clients. My personal life was far too important at the moment to effectively focus on my headhunter alter ego. I hung up the phone after a particularly draining call and put my head in my hands; a migraine was starting to push its way into my brain. Throwing down my pen in irritation, I picked up the phone to call Melissa, my surrogate big sister, to get her perspective on the emotional disaster that was slowly taking over my otherwise even-keeled life. Melissa and I met in high school at track practice when I was a freshman and she was a senior. Almost immediately, she adopted me as her protégé, and we had been friends ever since—even though she now lived and worked in Atlanta. I liked to refer to her as my own personal voice of reason. Plus the fact that she was so far away made it easier to tell her things that I hesitated to share with people I saw with more frequency.

"Good afternoon. MediaCom, Melissa speaking."

"Hi, it's me."

"Hey, what's up?"

"Well I just got back from the shrink…."

"How was it? Do you think it's helping?"

"I do. I still have a hard time completely opening up about some stuff, but it's made a huge difference. She said something today that I can't stop thinking about. She told me that I'm single, but I'm not available. Do you think that's true?"

Melissa paused. I could practically envision the wheels of her mind constructing a tactful answer—one that forced me to see the truth but at the same time did not hurt my feelings.

"Well when was the last time you saw or spoke to Matt?" she finally asked.

"We work in the same building and go to the same gym; that's not fair." I mentally patted myself on the back for evading the question.

She sighed. "When was the last time you slept with him?"

Dammit. She was good. I closed my eyes like a small child playing hide-and-seek.

"A few days ago?" I heard my voice come out sounding high-pitched and unsure.

"Dani! You did? Why didn't you tell me?"

Why had I kept it a secret even from her? I had no reasonable answer to offer. "I don't know!" I said helplessly. I really didn't. All I knew was that I needed to disentangle myself from this mess. I felt sick every time I lied to one of my friends and said I was staying in on a Friday night but was actually curled up next to Matt on his couch, drinking wine to alleviate my guilt.

After I hung up with Melissa, I spent the rest of the day in a fog, wondering how to gather the strength to just not answer the next time he called. I needed to just let it wither away and die, the way it should have months ago. The week continued on with no word from him, and then Friday arrived.

Ahhhh, Friday: everyone's favorite day of the workweek, but even more so for me in the summertime. Summer hours allowed me to leave early each Friday in order to get to my fabulous beach house every weekend. My main purpose in emptying my bank account to embark on these three-day adventures every week was to provide myself a solid distraction every Friday through Sunday. If I was down the shore having a blast with my girlfriends, I would not be thinking about or spending illicit time with Matt.

The clock hit one and I gathered up a few files and my bag. My cell phone buzzed on my way out the door. Text message.

Not just any text message. It read, "R u leaving? Call me if u are." My hand started shaking. That familiar weakness washed over me and, almost as if possessed, my fingers found their way to his number and hit send. It started ringing, and I mentally cursed myself for being such a jerk.

"Hey, are you leaving work?" Matt's voice could always lull me into submission. There was something so sexy about it; I could never explain it. He just always sounded like he was in bed and was calling to get you to hop in and join him.

"Yeah, I'm leaving. What's up?" I did my best to sound nonchalant. He wasn't fooled.

"Well I'm leaving too," he said slyly, "and I thought you could come by and hang out for a little bit before you left for the shore."

Here it was: my perfect opportunity to say *no fucking way* and not be this weak girl I had grown to despise. I felt like Carrie Bradshaw in that episode of *Sex and the City* when Mr. Big follows her into the elevator, trying to kiss her, and she keeps cursing at him until finally she acquiesces. My head was saying no a thousand times, but my heart—or the need to be irrational—won the battle at hand, making it quite clear that the war was far from over.

"Okay. I'll meet you at your house," I said numbly. I spent the drive over there trying to accomplish the feat of not thinking at all. I was not successful. All I could think about was my next session with Dr. Olsen—clearly having to admit what I did today—along with how late I was going to be getting down the shore. All of my friends were aware of my typical early Friday departures and might ask questions. Once again, there he was making my life needlessly difficult, and I was allowing him to do it.

When I arrived, we wasted no time. We barely said hello and

he was tugging my shirt over my head and half pulling, half carrying me to his bedroom. We never stopped kissing, not even to catch our breath. I was completely caught up and finally achieved a state where no thought existed except heat, passion, and our two bodies touching. Suddenly a voice penetrated the mindless haze I was in, but not Matt's voice—a child's voice. We both froze. There I was, completely naked, straddling Matt, neither one of us moving an inch, staring at each other, wondering about the source of the voice.

"I don't know, Grandma, Uncle Matt's car is in the driveway, but he's not answering. I keep knocking!"

Matt jumped up and started grabbing for his clothes. The voice came frighteningly close, right outside Matt's bedroom window. As Matt scrambled to get dressed, I tried to peek through the blinds to see who had interrupted us.

"My nephew," he mouthed at me, throwing my jeans at me while he struggled to put his pants back on. "I have to go let him in," he whispered. "Get dressed and then come out, or just wait here. I'll get rid of him."

Shit. Shit. I was panicked. All I needed was his nine-year-old nephew telling the whole family that he had caught us together in the middle of the day, especially given Matt's wack job of a brother C.J., with his strange jealousy, and his oddball of a mother who had never quite warmed up to me. Every conversation she and I had ever had centered around how Matt was "the most wonderful person" and that he "deserved the best of everything." He was clearly the favored child out of her four sons, which may have explained his partially deranged brother.

Matt had always said his nephew, Andrew, had a big mouth. At their last Christmas dinner, he had held up a Victoria's Secret catalog in front of everyone and asked Matt why it had my name and address on it and why certain pages were folded over. Although, I guess that is better than asking why the pages are sticky.

Where the hell is my shirt? Oh my God, it must be somewhere out in the living room. I looked around and grabbed a sleeveless shirt lying on the floor and threw it on. The two sides were gaping holes with a more than advantageous view of my naked chest. I heard Matt tell Andrew he wanted to show him something outside, so I dashed from his room into the bathroom. All this stress was making me have to pee. After I was done, I realized there was no way I could casually walk out in this outfit. I would just have to wait in the bathroom.

I heard them come back into the house, so I slowly pushed the door until it was almost completely shut, just so it would not make any noise. Then I went to the opposite end and sat on the bathroom counter, listening. Two seconds later the bathroom door started to open, and before I could react, I saw a black snout, two curious eyes, and pointed ears peek around the bathtub. "Oh thank God, Lucky, it's just you," I whispered. Lucky was their sweet, mixed-breed dog, so old that she could barely walk anymore. She shuffled towards me with her stiff gait, still wagging her tail despite her tumor-ridden body and arthritic legs. I knelt to pet her when all of a sudden she squatted. Turds the size of Chihuahuas started coming out. "Oh no, Lucky, Lucky, please honey, oh don't. Oh God. Please stop." The smell was horrendous, probably from all her medication. I started gagging. I pulled my shirt over my head. It did not help. I ran to the window, but it would not budge. The poor dog was in distress, going to different corners of the bathroom and letting more poop fly. I could barely breathe and was choking on the foul stench when I decided that I just needed to get the hell out of there. Who cared that my breasts were hanging out of the sides of the shirt? For once in my life I thanked God for only endowing me with a barely B-cup chest. Tentatively I started making my way around the poop to get to the door, when once again the door started to open. "Don't open it," I yelled, "there's…stuff everywhere."

"What are you talking about?" Matt peered in at me, confused, as he swung the door all the way open, right into one of Lucky's fresh piles, smearing it across the floor and along the bottom of the door. He looked at the poop. Then he looked at me. Then he looked at the poop again. Then he smiled. Then he started laughing. He pointed at me, shaking with laughter. "You…you were stuck in here with all this shit?" he sputtered.

I smiled. It was kind of funny. I looked around. It got funnier. I laughed so hard, tears began to roll down my face. Eventually our hysterics died down and I was again uncomfortably aware that I should not even be there with him. It was time to find my actual clothes and get the hell out of there. I hugged him goodbye when I was leaving.

"This was a bad idea. I shouldn't have come over today." My voice sounded clear and strong, not at all shaky. I was impressed with myself.

"Well, we didn't know you'd be trapped in the bathroom with poor Lucky." He always avoided any sort of significant conversation.

I shook my head. God forbid he ever had to take something seriously. He was just not equipped to handle it. "My shrink told me this week that I don't let myself take advantage of new opportunities because of this ongoing, back-and-forth thing that we have." I looked at him for a reaction.

"What the hell does that mean? It doesn't make any sense." He looked disinterested.

Even though he usually quizzed me about my shrink sessions and I told him straight out some of the things I discussed in therapy, he never wanted to believe our relationship was one of the reasons I had started going in the first place. It was unbelievable. He could not take responsibility for a damn thing.

"It means that *every* time I come here, I get shit on. Not just today." I looked at his face. You cannot make someone care. I know this. I couldn't make him care. Not the way I wanted him to. I felt my chest tighten. We must have said goodbye a million times by then, but I was the one who could not make it stick. He was just using me—I could feel it—but I did not want to see it. It hurt too much.

"I'm sorry about my nephew and Lucky! I didn't know any of this would happen. Why don't you call me later?" He had that devious look on his face again. "Or maybe skip the beach this weekend?" He smirked and grabbed both my arms to pull me close enough to feel his erection.

I pulled away from him and looked away. My entire being craved closeness with him. Pulling away took Herculean strength. It was definitely time to go. Not trusting my voice, I shook my head no and took a few more steps backward.

"Okay," he had that phony, miffed look on his face that he always got when he was trying to convince me to stay and I was protesting. I felt dejected and disappointed in myself all over again.

"Bye, Matt, I'll see ya." I walked quickly to my car without looking back.

"Bye, sexy!" he called out from behind me. "Text me something dirty later."

That summer flew. Maybe because I was dreading the lack of weekend plans once it was over, or because I was able to feel like I had a separate life down there, but those few months felt like they passed in an instant. Labor Day weekend arrived, and as I prepared to leave work on that last summer Friday, naturally, my phone rang. I rolled my eyes and put down my bags.

"Good afternoon, this is Danielle," I clicked the mouse to stop the computer from shutting down just in case the pain in the ass on the line needed to email me something.

"Hi, Danielle, it's Dr. Bernstein. How are you doing?"

My stomach dropped and a cold knot appeared in my stomach. Dr. Bernstein had only called me at work once before, to dispense of unpleasant test results. For a second, I felt like I might pass out. I swallowed past the lump in my throat. I needed to calm down; it could just be an anomaly like last time. "I'm fine, Dr. B, how are you?" I forced a note of fake cheerfulness into my voice.

"Good, but I need to talk to you about your Pap smear results. Unfortunately, they came up irregular again, so we're going to have to take the next step. I'm going to schedule you for cryosurgery next week. Basically what we do is freeze your cervix so that all the irregular cells sort of 'pop' off and leave your body, and...."

He kept talking, but I felt like I had gone deaf. I had sort of floated out of my body after the word *cryosurgery*. I thought back to the last phone call I had received from him months earlier, when I had first learned about this vague, potentially cancer-causing disease that would change everything.

Nine months earlier

"HPV? What is that?" My voice trembled and I clutched the phone tighter. This had to be some terrible illness since he was calling me at work.

"It's the human papillomavirus; it's very common," Dr. B reassured me. "It comes from skin-to-skin contact, so condoms don't always provide enough of a barrier to prevent it."

Common? I don't care if it's common*! I refuse to have an STD,* I raged silently to myself. This was not happening. I was the good girl. I had waited for the right guy, only slept with one person, and was *completely* monogamous, yet this was the reward? Bullshit! I should have gotten some kind of fucking plaque for making it through four years of college with my virginity intact! Half of my friends had lost track of how many sexual partners they had! I was on the verge of tears and felt like punching someone.

"Danielle, are you still there?" Dr. B's voice penetrated my inner rant. "I am going to make an appointment for you to come in for a colposcopy."

I paused. *A colposcopy?* "Ummm, Dr. Bernstein, isn't that to detect for colon cancer?"

He laughed, and I relaxed a little. "No, that's a colonoscopy. A colposcopy is a biopsy of the cervix. I'll make the appointment for next week. You are also going to want to inform your boyfriend about this."

I clutched the receiver again, feeling sick at the thought of telling Matt any of this.

Almost as if he sensed my discomfort, Dr. Bernstein said, "It's nothing to panic about; it's HPV—*not* HIV—but he's going to have to see a urologist so that the two of you don't keep passing it back and forth. Call me if you have any questions and I'll see you next week."

After I hung up, I started to craft an email to Matt. I wrote, "Hey, let's skip the gym after work and talk instead. I need to talk to you about something important." I stared at it and then deleted the whole thing. Knowing him, he would write back and ask what it was about, and I really did not want to discuss this over email, or actually ever. This was humiliating. I tapped my pen and racked my brain. Without warning, my eyes filled with tears, and I ran to the back office to hide from all my co-workers—except one.

"What's wrong?" Christina looked up at me with alarm and hung up her phone.

By then, tears were streaming freely down my face, and I couldn't even begin to make them stop. I sunk into the chair next to her and tried to get control of myself to explain why I was an emotional wreck. Her eyes were wide with concern, but she sat there patiently as I slowly calmed down. In our crazy office, she was the one unruffled presence who always kept a cool head. Plus she had been there from day one of my relationship with Matt and knew he was my first real…anything. A couple of years older than I, and a few more relationships worth of experience, she always seemed to have good advice for any issues I ever had with Matt. I took some deep breaths and finally spilled to her what was going on, as well as how I did not know how to tell Matt about it. I stared at my hands when I was done explaining, positive that she was thinking I was as disgusting as I felt.

"Dani, it's okay. Maybe the biopsy will show that nothing is wrong. You never know."

I looked up and she was nodding in accordance with her statement.

"I have friends," she continued, "who have been told something was 'irregular,' and on closer inspection, it was nothing. You just can't freak out about it. Try your best to not think about it until you go for your appointment. I know it's going to be hard, but you're just going to have to try to keep busy and put it out of your head. As for Matt, just tell him! It will be fine. Tell him that it might be nothing, if you think he'll panic, but your doctor is right: you need to tell him."

I couldn't believe how she was looking at me; it was as if nothing had changed. I felt like my life had been completely altered in the worst way possible, yet Christina was still imparting advice like it was any other day, not looking at me any differently. I felt a small rush of hope. If she did not find me repulsive for being diagnosed with this…this *disease*, maybe it really wasn't as bad as I thought. Talking to her at least made me feel slightly more ready to drop the bomb on Matt.

I got back to my desk and, after a slight hesitation, grabbed the phone and dialed his work number.

"Matt Ryan," he sounded so professional. I loved talking to him at work.

"Hi, it's me," I played with the phone cord, my stomach in knots. "How are you?"

"Hey!" he sounded so happy to hear from me; I almost chickened out. "I was just thinking about you. I'm good. How's your day been?"

I paused, wondering if I should just wait until after work to do this. "I have to tell you something…" I took a deep breath, "my doctor called today and he said that um, he said that, well he said that my test results were irregular." I waited, listened, but apparently I had rendered him speechless, so I forged ahead. "I need to get a biopsy, but the good thing is that it's possible that nothing is wrong at all! Which would be the ideal situation, so let's hope for that. Oh and he thinks that you need to see a urologist." I said the last part in a rush. I was fairly sure Matt did not even have a general physician, never mind a urologist.

"Okay...what exactly is wrong with you?" he said slowly.

I cringed. That's what I was afraid of: the assumption that something was "wrong" with me. Not exactly a welcome stigma to carry around. I felt a little stung that he did not immediately ask how I was feeling, if I was all right, etc. I shook it off; this call was obviously unexpected, and could I really blame him for not reacting the way I wanted?

I offered what little information I had about HPV, and as I was explaining it, I realized that I was altering my tone and choice of words to calm *him* down and make *him* feel better, the same way Christina had done for me ten minutes earlier. Something was nagging me in the back of my head. Wasn't he being a little selfish? At that moment, shouldn't he have been more concerned about *me*? I ended the conversation and sat at my desk, very unsettled. Why had I tried so hard to comfort him when I was the one who felt scared and in need of reassurance? I pushed my uncertainty out of my head. The last thing I needed on top of this was to be questioning our relationship. He was just caught off guard, and I was overreacting. Yes. That's all it was.

A few days later when I succumbed to the colposcopy, it was ironically Valentine's Day. The night before, Matt had taken me to dinner and given me a beautiful necklace, and we both carefully avoided the topic of where I was headed the next day. I sat in the waiting room, fiddling with my new necklace, wondering what the colposcopy would entail. Just like a regular exam but a little bit longer?

"Danielle?" A nurse was standing at the door with my file in her hands. I nervously picked up my bag and followed her to the exam room. "You can undress from the waist down," she directed, "and Dr. Bernstein will be right in to see you."

I nodded my understanding and waited for her to shut the door behind her. I removed my jeans and underwear, wrapped the paper gown around my waist, and sat on the exam table. Not two minutes later, Dr. Bernstein walked in with three people in tow. One was a nurse I recognized, but I had never seen the other two before, both who were dressed in scrubs.

"How are you, kiddo?" Dr. Bernstein boomed, and I smiled.

"Could be better," I announced with a laugh as I moved to lie back on the table.

"We'll get you in and out today as quick as we can," he promised. "These are two medical students who are observing today. They'll be watching me perform the biopsy."

"Okay." I had not really prepared my vagina for an audience, but it looked like there was no choice in the matter.

Dr. Bernstein started to insert the speculum, and I felt the familiar pressure. I could see that he was using some sort of contraption to look inside, and it was not comfortable, especially when he turned to start explaining himself to the medical students. I started to sweat and wished that I had taken my heavy sweater off along with my jeans.

"Okay, so you see those four spots that are showing up?" Dr. B was asking the med students. "Danielle, I've applied a dye to your cervix to see what shows up, and I'm now going to scrape those four spots and biopsy them to either confirm or rule out the HPV diagnosis."

"Okay," I gasped. "Are you almost done?" My body continuously and painfully bucked the speculum, knowing intuitively that a foreign metal object did not belong in there. And it felt as if Dr. B was reaching so far up to scrape my cervix that I could feel his reach in my stomach.

"All done," he announced a few minutes later. "I'm inserting a surgical tampon. You're going to have cramping and bleeding for the next few hours. Change the tampon tonight before you go to bed, okay?"

"Okay," I murmured. I could already feel the cramping; it was really nauseating. I left there that day thinking there could not be many things in this world worse than a colposcopy. When I called Matt to update him, he interrupted me to say his stomach was upset and he needed to call me back. Really supportive.

A week later, the office called to say that the biopsy had shown up negative for HPV and that I just needed to schedule a followup exam in six months as a precautionary measure. Matt was beyond thrilled. So was I, but something about the way he handled the whole thing left a bad taste in my mouth. And while I still did not say anything, I found myself looking at him differently—perhaps my very first traces of cynicism starting to emerge.

* * *

I smiled sadly, remembering that whole mess. Back then I had not been capable of calling him out on anything, and he knew it. That was not even the first time he had so flagrantly disregarded my feelings, which proved that I should have known better by that point. Now I had to subject my nether regions to this thing called cryosurgery, and Matt and I were only speaking when he was trying to get me to come over and take off my clothes. The thought of telling my mom made me queasy as I pictured how the shock and disappointment would register on her face. Tears began to burn the back of my eyes. Convinced that my friends would treat me differently if they knew my doctor suspected I had an STD, I had barely told anyone about the biopsy so many months ago. Who could I ask to drive me to the procedure?

Just then, Christina walked by my desk and plunked down a bag of gummy peach rings from the candy store downstairs. "I ate half already," she laughed, "so you finish them."

I laughed half-heartedly and aimlessly began to chew on one without tasting it. All of a sudden, my eyes widened. I shook my head at how dense I was and jumped out of my chair to run after her.

A week later, I walked stiffly into the waiting room of Dr. Bernstein's office, Christina in tow. The receptionist smiled sympathetically at me when I signed in, obviously fully aware of the reason for my visit. Mentally I had been preparing myself for this for the past week, but then last night had ruined my optimistic outlook in a matter of five minutes. I shook my head, trying to remove the painful images that were glaringly burned into my brain, and felt my fists clench in my attempt to block it all out. Tears would not even form this time. I felt empty. Dully, I sat next to Christina, waiting for my name to be called.

I had assumed that I would be at my most anxious the night before the cryosurgery appointment. The nervous anticipation combined with not knowing exactly what to expect was bound to make it an awful night. Fortunately, my friend Joe had purchased a block of tickets for a huge group of my friends to see Coldplay in concert at Madison Square Garden. I could not have dreamed up a better distraction—except that as we arrived at MSG and were walking through the main doors, I saw Matt right in front of me with a group of his coworkers, his arm familiarly around the shoulders of another girl. I did not even realize that I had stopped walking until a few seconds later when tons of people brushing by me jostled me into awareness. Instinctively I clutched at my best friend Elise's arm. She was mid-conversation with someone else and glanced up at me questioningly.

I watched Matt throw his head back and laugh at whatever the girl said to him. She then playfully shoved him away and pretended to start running. Still laughing, he darted after her and grabbed her back. I recognized her. She worked in his office. He introduced her to me once and later mentioned that he hooked up with her a few times before he met me. I held on to Elise for dear life. I felt like I might explode from the hurt that was making the rounds through my entire body. I wanted to die. Instead I ran to the nearest bathroom and vomited up everything I had just eaten at the Sbarro across the street. In retrospect, the spaghetti had been a very poor choice. I sat on the disgusting, bacteria-laden tiled floor and leaned my head on the toilet paper dispenser. The coolness of the metal felt like ice against my flushed forehead. It felt like hours before I was able to pry myself off the floor and return to my seat. I prayed for the concert to fly by so I could just go home and be alone, with no one there to see me fall apart. Somehow I managed to placate my friends with a wan smile and some intermittent clapping for the next few hours. I cannot even recall the band's playlist.

I flipped through a magazine in the waiting room, barely read anything in it, then picked another one. Flipped through that too without looking.

Christina sighed, "Dani, you have *got* to relax."

Relax. Sure. Because it is so *normal to get your cervix frozen.* I felt completely on edge, like if they did not call me in the next few minutes, I might just flee the place altogether. I would be fine, I reasoned in my head. Go to GNC, pick up some vitamins, and fix this HPV right up. Just as I was half convinced that this was my best course of action, the door opened and Maria, my favorite nurse, called for me.

I lay on the table in my paper gown, my feet in the stirrups. My legs were trembling, and all my muscles felt tense and tight. Dr. B and Maria came in, Dr. B with his usual "How's it goin', kiddo?" greeting and Maria with her sweet smile and calm demeanor. He explained that he would be putting in the speculum as if it were a regular pap smear and then inserting something called a CryoProbe, which would allow cold liquid nitrogen to flow onto my cervix and freeze the abnormal cells there. After a few minutes of freezing, we would take a break and then insert the CryoProbe one more time for another minute or two. For the first thirty seconds I did not feel a thing, and then all of a sudden I felt a cold sensation spreading throughout my gut. It was uncomfortable but not terrible. I started to relax a little bit. Before I knew it, it was time for the break. Dr. B said he would be back in five minutes and told me to try to relax. I lay there with the speculum still inside me, uncomfortable as it always was, but then the cramping started to kick into high gear. My entire abdomen felt cold, and sharp pains were starting to come in waves. I began to sweat as I bore down against them. I felt nauseous and tried to call out for somebody to come, but my throat was too dry. In the time Dr. B and Maria were gone, it felt like days had passed. When they returned, I wanted to tell them I could not possibly do one more round, but I did not have the nerve. I just nodded when they asked if I was ready, then winced when they reinserted the CryoProbe. Silently I started to cry. I turned my head so they would not see me, but I could not stop myself. Matt was out with another girl. He was being playful and cute with her, probably sleeping with her, and I was here with my legs in the air, embracing an ice storm with my vagina. She was not even attractive! A total "but-her-face" as my friend Mikey would have called her. I cried at the unfairness of it all. *Nobody deserves this*, I thought with a sudden flash of anger—a welcome emotional departure from the anxiety, fear, and panic that had wracked my brain and body thus far.

After we left the doctor's office, Christina deposited me at my parents' house to spend the rest of the day in bed. "Are you sure you're okay?" She looked at me worriedly. "You're really pale."

I smiled weakly, trying to reassure her. "I'll be fine. I smell like freezer burn, but I'm fine." She and I laughed together. Although I was joking, I really did detect a faint smell reminiscent of freezer burn. *Wonderful*. Just what I needed on top of everything else. I slowly let myself into the house and lay on the couch. I had thought I would fall asleep from sheer exhaustion the minute I got home, but even with my eyes closed, my mind would not relax, racing over the events of the past week: the phone call, the concert, this morning's appointment. I picked up my phone and called Matt. Half expecting to get his voicemail, I was a little surprised when he answered after the second ring.

"Hello?" He sounded kind of sleepy.

"Hi, it's me. Why aren't you at work?"

"I took the day off because I went to see Coldplay last night." He yawned.

"Yeah I saw you last night." I paused, trying to decide what to say next. "You were wearing a green shirt." *Shit.* That was not what I wanted to say.

"Tan."

"What?"

"I was wearing a tan shirt." He sounded amused and I had an uncontrollable urge to slap him. My previous flash of anger at the doctor's office began to erupt—and Mount Vesuvius has nothing on a woman scorned with a frozen tundra where her cervix used to reside.

"Tan, green, whatever. I also saw you with that girl—the one from your office who you used to fuck." I felt vulgar using those words but at the same time could not help myself. He stayed silent. I took this as confirmation that he was seeing her again. "Do you know where I was this morning? No, you don't, because you don't care about anyone but yourself. You dirty, diseased piece of shit. Do you even know what I had to go through today? Do you even *know?*" I felt my voice shrilly reaching the point of hysteria and took a breath to calm down. He coughed uncomfortably and still remained silent. "I was at my doctor's office having something called cryosurgery. Do you know what that is? Of course you don't. I didn't know what it was until a week ago. Basically, I had to go get *rid* of the disease you gave me with your dirty dick." My chest was tight and heaving, but I could not stop now; the words were just spilling out and I could neither stop them nor censor them. Even in my tirade I knew I was not being fair. I had loved him and wanted to make love to him all those times, but he hurt me and I needed to retaliate—*had* to retaliate. "Do you know how sick I feel right now? I've been throwing up from stress and you're out screwing other girls and passing your disease along its merry way. Don't you even care what your actions cause? Does it even matter to you?"

"Yes," he said quietly. "Of course it matters."

I waited for more, and when he fell silent again, I continued my ranting. "You didn't even apologize," I felt my voice breaking. "You just left me to clean up your mess. You took no responsi-bili—"

"Okay!" he burst out. "I'm sorry, all right? I didn't intend for any of this to happen!"

"I don't care about your *intention*, Matthew! That's not an apology! No one *intends* for this to happen! But I needed you to face it with me like an adult instead of running away. You are thirty years old! Grow the fuck up!" Now I was exhausted and felt sick again. I just could not win. It was clear that it had all been one-sided. I realized he had been able to dismiss me far too easily. That was not love; that was convenience. And now we had made our beds. I would be sleeping in mine alone now, and he would always have company in his who would find out much too late that his recklessness would wreak havoc on their health.

"What do you want from me?" he asked tiredly.

"I don't want anything." I sighed. But I was far from telling the truth, and we both knew it. I had no idea what it was that I wanted. Closure? Apologies? Groveling? All three? Regardless, it was clear that I was not going to get any of it. He started to speak again and I just hung up. I thought that would be it for us, but I wondered how it was that we had managed to get to this place of anger, resentment, and pain.

two

A KISS IS STILL A KISS

*"A kiss is a lovely trick designed by nature to stop speech
when words become superfluous."* —*Ingrid Bergman*

The beginning is always easy. First kisses and passion. Staying up late on the phone because neither one of you can bear to hang up. Total bliss. Matt wandered into my life when I least expected it. But I believe that is what everyone says. Still pretty fresh out of college, I had started working at my first "real" job, with a salary and 401(k). The company was Hamilton & Stone, a boutique recruiting firm that specialized in finance, located in the small town of Pearl River, New York. Walking into my office building every morning was how I first noticed him. I almost cannot explain what it was that initially drew me to him. There was one particular morning that I caught him walking into the building alone rather than with the usual harem of females who I could only assume were his coworkers. His expression looked like his mind was a million miles away and he almost seemed a little lost to me, mirroring how I felt at the time. I had no idea if I was in the right job or if I even knew what the right job would be for me—typical post-college confusion. That morning, we did not even exchange a word, but I was struck by a precognition that we were soon going to know each other. To this day I do not know how I knew that with such certainty, but over the next couple of years, my intuition proved correct both in ways I will never forget and ways I wish I could completely eradicate from my memory.

Our first real conversation took place in the small fitness center on the first floor of our massive office building. In the beginning, I had disregarded him and every other guy who worked out there and had given me the standard once-over. I had no interest in flirtations at the gym; I just wanted to get in and get out after a long day at work. Adapting to this new world of cubicles and one-hour lunches instead of lenient college professors and afternoon naps had proven to be a huge undertaking. I did not feel ready to entertain the idea of meeting someone and developing a relationship when I did not yet have a firm grasp on what I was even doing with my life. Slowly though, we started to have these mini-conversations by the water fountain. Casual topics. He had just gotten back from a trip to Thailand, I was taking a trip to Las Vegas and he had never been…. Nothing of real substance was discussed, but he was starting to grow on me. His little quips made me laugh since his sense of humor was right in line with my own, and his smile was so engaging that after a few weeks of talking, a full-fledged crush had taken hold of me. I caught myself hoping that I would see him every time I went to work out, and if he failed to show, disappointment inevitably followed.

Coincidentally, my birthday was coming up, giving me the perfect excuse to invite him somewhere where I could actually talk to him in an outfit that was not dripping with sweat, in a place without elliptical machines. I spent days planning how to casually invite him.

"Hi!" I smiled at Matt, hoping he did not notice how nervous I was or how my *hi* had been a little overly cheerful.

"Hey, Danielle," he smiled back and put down the dumbbells that he had been using. "How's your day been?"

I have no idea what it is, but when someone I am interested in says my name, I get a chill that runs right through every part of me. It is delicious. "It's been good," I asserted, copping what I hoped was a super casual pose. "I was wondering…" I paused trying to strike the right balance of nonchalance, "if you're free on Saturday night. I'm going out in the city for my birthday, and there's a drink special for thirty-five dollars, and it's going to be really fun, and you can invite whomever you want, and…." I caught myself rambling and just stopped. Either he would say yes or no. I gave it a shot. I realized I was holding my breath.

"Sure, I'll come," he smiled. "Where is it? Can I bring my brother and a couple friends?"

"Of course!" I managed to stutter out. "Here is the invite; bring whomever. The more the merrier." Elation does not even begin to describe how I was feeling. It had been so long since I had been excited about a guy. And we were finally going to see each other outside of this stupid office building! I nervously threw my hand out to give him the little card with martini decorations on it. "Okay, so all the information is there. Seriously, bring whomever you want and…umm…that's it?" *That wasn't a question*, I mentally admonished myself.

"Sounds good, D." He leaned in extremely close and looked me up and down. I stopped breathing. Truly. All air stopped going in and out. Then he whispered, "And try to clean up a little for your party, huh? Shower, wear something besides sweatpants. I'm sure you can figure it out."

Laughing, I punched him in the shoulder, and he danced away grinning wickedly.

"Well here's your opportunity to finally see me looking like something other than the poster child for Nike," I retorted, smiling bigger than ever. "You better be there," I warned, only half-joking but loving how he was flirting with me. It felt like flirting. He *had* to be flirting.

"Just be ready to party," he smiled and squeezed my arm. "See you Saturday."

I watched him walk out of the gym, my entire arm tingling and fervently wishing I could fast forward to Saturday night.

"So where is he?" Elise looked skeptical as we both checked our cell phones for the time. 1:45 a.m. I looked up and scanned the bar again, hoping that I would focus in on Matt's tall physique in order to refute the possibility that he had just not shown up. I felt a sick twist in my gut and checked my phone one more time for a text message or missed call. Nothing. I had put my number on the invitation, so he had to have it. My mind searched for possibilities as to why he did not even call: Car accident? He lost the invite? The sick feeling enveloped my whole body as I watched some of my friends talk to Elise in the corner of the bar. She was shaking her head and shrugging her shoulders and they had sympathetic looks on their faces. I could just picture it: another potential guy for Dani bites the dust would be what they were saying. The thought of their pity made me want to throw up. Instead I reached around my friend Doug at the bar, took the shot he was in the middle of paying for, and threw it down my throat. Bleccch, it was Jägermeister. I gagged and turned to chug my beer as a reprieve while Doug looked around in confusion for the shot that had disappeared—my cue to wander away from the bar.

I cursed myself mentally as I wandered back over to the dance floor where my friends were rocking out. I had been looking forward to hanging out with Matt all day and was even too nervous and excited to eat. But here it was, almost two in the morning, and I was not naïve enough to think that he was going to show up now. I let my alcoholic haze carry me through the rest of the party and had a great time with my friends. But I refused to believe that Matt would be so callous. *He had promised*, I thought desperately, and he had not called to say otherwise. I shook my head, trying to force all thoughts and emotions over him out of my mind. I would have to let my disappointment seep in the next morning— along with my hangover.

"So he just didn't show up?"

I winced and rubbed my forehead. It was the next morning, I had a pounding headache from my party, and my mom was subjecting me to an interrogation that I really was not equipped to handle.

"Yes," I answered wearily.

"Well then he's not interested in you," my mom stated bluntly.

"You don't know that for sure," I said testily. Who the hell did she think she was? She hadn't even met the guy!

"Well if he really liked you he would have made it last night," she said with superiority.

My crankiness was in full swing now. "Maybe he had some kind of emergency," I protested. "Or he lost the invitation."

"Oh Dani." Now she looked at me sympathetically. "You're smarter than that! Has he called you to say why he didn't make it?" she asked.

"No," I said sullenly.

She raised her eyebrows. "Guys who like you—and I mean *really* like you—they will always make the effort to see you if they know you want to see them. Your father drove down to the beach twice in one day from Brooklyn once, and you know what?"

"What?" I humored her, even though I knew the answer.

"Your father *hates* the beach!" she declared triumphantly, having proved her point.

I buried my face in my hands. Guys were not like that anymore, were they? The ones my age did not seem to have a chivalrous bone in their body.

"Hey! Hey, Danielle! How was your party?" I tensed. I had avoided Matt at the gym for a couple of days now, hoping my disappointment and humiliation would be less apparent after a few days had passed. I still could not decide whether to be friendly and pretend I did not care or to act a little cooler towards him. He did not owe me anything, one side of my brain argued. Just the respect and courtesy of acting like an adult, the other side shouted. And to my annoyance, my mother's words were echoing in my mind over and over. Slowly I turned around from the pull-down bar to face him, using all my strength to project a neutral tone of voice.

"Hi, Matt." In that second, I made the decision to be a little distant. "So many people showed up; it was really great. You missed a fun party." Well that was neutral. I turned back to the pulldown bar. "Sorry you couldn't make it." Good. Offhanded and over the shoulder. Why should I be so upset anyway? It was not like anything had ever happened, I reasoned. He was neither my boyfriend nor knew me long enough to be a close friend. Hell, he was not even a hookup. But the rationalizations were not making me feel any better. Simply put, I felt stupid. I had gone out on a limb because I had really started to like him, but he had left me feeling like a schmuck.

"I'm so sorry I didn't make it. I really wanted to, I swear. I was even coming with a whole group of guys, but after the place we were going to crash at fell through, nobody wanted to drive, so it just didn't work out. So that whole night kind of sucked because all I wanted was to go to your party."

I stayed silent with my back still to him. I was confused. No place to crash? No one wanted to drive? He was twenty-eight years old, not twenty. If he really wanted to come, why didn't he just drive himself and cut himself off after a few drinks? My mother was right: if he really liked me, none of that would have gotten in the way of him coming to my party. The rejection I felt on Saturday was coming back full force. *Obviously getting drunk with his friends was a bigger priority*, I thought dejectedly. I had to get out of there before he could see how much it all really bothered me.

"Okay, well I'm all done here," I forced a bright note into my voice. "It's all yours; I need to get home." I turned around so quickly I almost tripped over my own feet but caught myself and walked towards the locker room with barely a glance back at him. Disappointment tightened my chest, and I quickened my pace.

"Okay, have a good night," I heard him say from somewhere behind me. He sounded distinctly unsure of himself, and I took a small amount of pleasure in it.

A few weeks went by, and I finally stopped cursing my stupidity. I even got over my discomfort at the gym and stopped avoiding him so much but was still careful to keep my distance. My hopes had been just a little too high before anything had even happened, so I would not allow myself to even consider him as anything other than someone I said hello to a few times a week. Every time he got a little too playful or friendly, it was always time for me to call it a night. He seemed aware that something had changed between us but continued to make attempts to draw me into conversation. I would oblige, then catch myself and make excuses for my departure. I noticed that he looked disappointed or confused on more than one occasion, but I could not have it any other way. He just sent too many mixed messages. Then a random rainy day changed everything.

I remember every single thing about that day. It was not a typical summer thunderstorm on July 12, 2004. The rain poured out of grey, overcast skies all morning and afternoon. I was at the gym after work, as usual, and telling a few of the regulars about how I had gotten lost driving around in Ramsey, New Jersey, and Suffern, New York, over the weekend.

Matt was listening and chimed in while lying on the weight bench. "I live in Suffern. What were you doing in Suffern?"

"I have an appointment at this spa called The Fountain one day after work. It's in Ramsey and I was trying to figure out how to get there from this building," I explained. I had not forgotten that he lived in Suffern. I wondered again like I had the day before if I had passed his house during my adventure up that way. Then I squashed the thought. Crushes die hard.

"I know how you can get there."

I looked up at him surprised.

He was standing over me, nodding his head. "Yes, I can definitely tell you how to get there; it's basically the route I take home every day. Super easy."

"Thanks!" This was great; I could write down the directions from him instead of attempting Mapquest and getting lost again. Once I was done with my workout, I grabbed a pen and some paper out of my bag and wandered back over to the ab bench where Matt was doing crunches. "Could you write down the directions for me?"

He sat up and reached for the pen, then made a face. "Shit… I'm sorry, Danielle, I just realized I don't know street names." He looked at me apologetically.

I stood there with a fixed smile, still holding the piece of paper and feeling like a moron. My *God*! What was it with this guy? Why did it always feel like I was some kind of bumbling fool around him? I took the pen back and just shrugged with forced casualness. "No biggie, I'll just Mapquest it again." I started to walk away, once again feeling like a marionette. I let him pull my strings, I danced, and people laughed—or at least they would if they could see how idiotic it made me behave.

"Wait! Maybe I could actually show you the way to go? You could follow me and I'll take you the route I know."

I turned around again and looked at him. I hated that just the fact that he had offered to do that completely altered my mood. *He still has an effect on me*, I thought in annoyance. "Are you sure?" I asked cautiously. "I don't want you to go out of your way for this. I really can just go back on the Internet."

"No, it's not out of the way at all. Just wait here; I'm going to go get my bag."

I waited in the hallway, leaning on the wall just outside of the gym. I concentrated on feeling absolutely nothing so my face would not betray me when he came back out. This was not even a big deal; he was just making a friendly overture. He walked out and we headed to the parking lot together.

As we started to split off towards our cars, he stopped for a second. "I should give you my number, just in case we lose each other."

My mouth fell open. "Right!" I was quick to agree. "The weather being so crappy and all…." *Whyyyy* was he doing this to me now? At a time when I had gotten over my resentment (sort-of) from his no-show at my birthday and been trying to accept the fact that nothing was going to happen. I felt heat rising in my cheeks as he put his head close to mine to watch me program his number into my phone. My hand shook. I finished programming it in and headed for my car, shouting, "Don't drive too fast."

Following him through the windy streets in the pouring rain, I could not ignore the giddy feeling I felt from him offering to do this. I had carefully spent the last few weeks convincing myself that the window of opportunity to be more than friends had closed the night of my birthday. But that careful façade I had constructed was starting to fall apart as a small ray of hope once again built inside me. After what felt like a million twists and turns in completely unfamiliar towns, I decided to call him and find out where the hell he was leading me.

"Hey!" Matt sounded completely surprised when he answered.

"So just wondering," I began coyly, "are you leading me into the woods somewhere to murder me, and no one will ever hear from me again or find my body?"

He laughed. "I know, it's totally all these little side roads, but trust me, I'll get you there. I promise I'm not kidnapping you and locking you in my basement. Although…my basement is not far from where we're going to be," he added thoughtfully.

"Well, if you're in the basement with me, I guess I wouldn't mind…" I teased, then held my breath, not sure if I was being a little too forward.

"Oh really?"

Yay! His tone of voice was just as flirty as mine. I smiled to myself. *Finally!* We fell easily into conversation, talking and flirting the rest of the way to The Fountain; I was actually disappointed when we finally pulled into the parking lot and had to hang up. I watched him pull a U-turn in the parking lot and pull up alongside my car. We both rolled down our windows and smiled at each other.

"So…um, thank you? I hope I didn't make you go too far out of your way to do this."

"No, don't worry. I seriously live about a mile from here," he carelessly gestured out the window with his arm. "It was no problem at all." He smiled again and I felt myself blush.

In that moment, I knew that he did not want to just drive off either. Something was happening and we both were too curious to not pursue it. Even with the driving rain pelting my face and rolling uncomfortably down my neck through my open window, I could not pull myself away. We again naturally fell into conversation as if we were sitting in a restaurant. Periodically we would laugh about how ridiculous we probably looked, hanging out our windows in a random parking lot, deep in conversation. Over an hour passed without one lull or awkward silence. I looked up at the grey sky and made a face.

"Can you believe that it hasn't stopped raining for even a second? I'm getting soaked over here. How about you?" I looked at him, mentally kicking myself for sounding like I wanted to get going. Leaving was the only thing I did *not* want to do.

"I'm a little damp, nothing I can't handle. The rain has its good points though."

"Oh yeah?" I shot him a disbelieving look. "What exactly are its good points when its summertime and supposed to be sunny and beautiful outside?"

"I don't know," he laughed. "Fun stuff like mud sliding."

"Mud sliding? Actually, that is fun," I mused with a grin, "but I haven't done that since college. I've got a better one: how about swimming in the rain?"

"Nope," he shook his head with a wicked grin, "swimming *naked* in the rain."

"Whoa!" I giggled, feeling silly. "That's not bad, but then again, nothing—I repeat, *nothing*—is better than making out in the rain."

"Making out in the rain is pretty good," he conceded. "I'll give you that."

"Pretty good?" I exclaimed. "It's *great*. In fact, I think we should take advantage and make out right now." I looked him right in the eyes to gauge his reaction. I had stunned myself; I could not believe I had it in me to be that bold. He looked surprised, interested, and skeptical all at once.

"You're not serious?" he asked. "You're joking, right?"

I shook my head no and, making a split-second decision, proceeded to get out of my car and walk the five feet over to his car. I bent down and studied his face—actually got close enough to feel the tangible chemistry resonating between us—then smiled and started to walk back to my car.

"Wait!"

I turned around and looked at him expectantly.

"Where are you going?" he stammered out.

"I just needed to show you that I was serious," I shrugged and opened my car door, "but if you're not interested, that's okay. I just thought it might be fun." Inside I was smiling; I knew now that he was interested, but he had to make a *little* effort. I heard the sound of a car door opening and turned around to see him getting out of his car. A thrill raced through me. I leaned against my car and watched him walk towards me. He looked a little uncertain, but I felt a little uncertain, so at least we were on the same page. He stopped within an inch of me and we stared at each other for what felt like ages but could not have been more than a few seconds. I wanted to kiss him in that moment more than I have ever wanted anything in my entire life. At the same time, I was afraid to break the spell I was under: just standing there, absorbing his closeness, his scent, the anticipation of it all.

"Oh hell," he muttered and just grabbed and kissed me. He tasted like summer and passion; it was excitingly new and weirdly familiar at the same time. The kiss continued on and on; it was downright electric. Intoxicating. My knees buckled. My right foot might have even done that pop thing that only happens in movies. Weakly, I leaned back and gazed at him. His eyes were penetrating, and he looked as off balance as I felt. "You're an amazing kisser," he finally said.

"You're not so bad yourself," I said softly, not trusting my voice not to shake. Before I could say anything else, we were suddenly kissing again, his hands in my hair, then around me pulling me tighter to his chest. I felt like my mouth was glued to his; I could not even come up for air. Virgin status aside, I had kissed *a lot* of boys over the years, and this was hands down the best kiss I had ever experienced. When he released me, I looked up at him, dazed. He smiled down at me. "Mmmmm, I knew you'd be good," I announced knowingly. It was the truth; he was every bit the kisser that I had imagined him to be.

"What do you mean?" he laughed. "You knew I'd be good at molesting your face in the rain in a public parking lot?"

"Exactly," I exclaimed. "I have always imagined letting you molest my face." He threw his head back and laughed and I smiled. It was so comfortable, I noticed: just being around him. I wanted to savor this…this feeling of being with someone who was just getting to know me, and I him, but somehow with the comfort that usually came with years of knowledge—intimate knowledge. It was such an alien feeling, I was afraid of losing it. It was *so* powerful. I could almost believe in things like destiny today. Then Matt bent his head again, and I ceased to believe in anything except how damn good his tongue felt in my mouth.

Hours must have gone by—or at the very least a good twenty minutes. Reluctantly, I pulled out of his arms and looked in at the clock on my dashboard. *7:45? Oh shit!* We had been here for an hour and fifteen minutes. My mom was going to kill me. I *hated* living at home again. I missed college where I could come and go as I pleased, no questions asked—least of all by a constantly overwrought mother who always dreamed up horrific scenarios of where I might be if she had not heard from me in a couple hours. I buried my face in his chest. He smelled like a combination of rain, sweat, and a little bit of cologne. Really masculine. I smiled. Then he put his chin on top of my head, causing me to frown. I hoped he wasn't smelling my hair! It probably reeked after being at the gym. Suddenly self-conscious, I pulled back again and looked up at him. He looked like he was not ready to be done with me, and I shivered a little—partly from the rain, partly from the excitement of being held by someone who obviously wanted me so much. I could even feel the…*physical* evidence and found myself blushing again but also reveling in it. *This must be what it feels like*, I thought. I finally could see what it felt like to want to be as physically close to someone as possible. He leaned his head down to kiss me again, and I closed my eyes and giddily waited for it. I had never been so attracted to anyone in my entire life.

I drove home in the rainy darkness, gently touching my mouth. It was swollen and sensitive from kissing Matt for so long. I had this inward glow, and I felt like I had reached the pinnacle of happiness that afternoon. This day would go down in the annals of my limited romantic history. My phone was going off. I picked it up and flipped it open as I rolled my eyes in exasperation.

"Dani? Where are you?" My mother's voice, worried but accusing at the same time.

"I'm on my way home, Mom," I sighed. "I stayed at the gym longer than usual and then…then I ran some errands," I improvised.

"It's dark though! And rainy! You better be careful driving," she warned. "Are you using your hands-free? You can get a ticket for being on your cell phone, you know."

"I know! Mom, I am twenty-three. I can drive in the rain. I can drive in the dark. I can drive in the sun, the snow, hail, sleet, wind, *whatever*." I shook my head, knowing she was going to get upset, but she had to realize, I was not in high school anymore. I had a college degree and I could not stand being treated like an eight-year-old.

"Well…there's no need to get fresh, Danielle." I could hear the hurt in her voice, and then I felt guilty. She only called me Danielle when she was mad or upset. I needed to move out ASAP. This was just not working. I sighed again.

"Sorry, Mom, I'll be home soon. I'm just going to swing by Elise's for ten minutes on the way." After all, I had to share the details of my clandestine, rainy afternoon with *someone*.

"Okay, well say hello to her parents, and don't interrupt their din—"

"Phone's cutting out, can't hear you!" I shouted and hung up. Talking to her was such an ordeal sometimes.

While driving to Elise's parents' house, the excitement of finally kissing Matt took hold of me again, and I could not get the stupid, shit-eating grin off my face. I sang along to every song on the radio. I was just starting to belt out some Pat Benatar when my phone beeped. I flipped it open and saw there was a text message from Matt: *That was a lot of fun. Do it again sometime? ;-)* My smile got bigger. Trying to text back and watch the road in the rain and dark proved to be a challenge, and I made a wrong turn. As I tried to make a K-turn, I crashed into a curb. *Good thing the Ford Escape sits high off the ground!* I sat there, put the car in park, finished the text, and looked at myself in the rearview mirror. "Calm down," I said sternly to my reflection. "You may have kissed the guy today who you've had a crush on for months, but you don't get to do it again if you get yourself killed on the way home!" Then I grinned broadly and cracked up. Anyone driving by must have thought I was a lunatic; there I was on a dead-end, suburban street, in a mini-SUV that was turned in towards the curb, with one tire over it on someone's lawn, laughing to myself and singing to the radio. A long time ago, someone told me that you should reserve five minutes every day for silliness. I was probably at my quota for the year.

I pulled into Elise's driveway, having just sent her a text that I was dropping by for a couple of minutes to tell her some big news. She was waiting for me at the door. I got out of the car and walked towards her, still unable to stop smiling.

"What is it?" she demanded. "What happened?"

I grabbed her and dragged her upstairs, yelling a hello to her parents on the way. I flopped on her bed and sighed dramatically.

She carefully shut the door and perched next to me on the bed. "If you don't tell me right this second…" she warned with a smile.

I rolled up in a sitting position and clutched her arm. "I kissed him!" I whispered excitedly. "Like full-on-totally-made-out-for-practically-an-hour-in-the-pouring-rain kissed him!" I collapsed back on the bed and then announced, "It was amaaaazing." I giggled, feeling like I was in high school again but struck by how much it affected me. In the past a kiss with a new guy could hardly get me to swoon, but I was still feeling some major sparks and a good half hour, forty minutes, had passed since I reluctantly had removed my mouth from his. It was not just a kiss, I realized—it was a promise. It had *felt* like a promise—of something new and amazing and more exciting to come.

"Wait! Wait, you don't mean…? You kissed him? Shut *up*!" She smacked my leg in disbelief. "How did this happen? I thought you weren't going to bother with him after he didn't show up for your birthday last month?"

I winced. Leave it to Elise to point that out. In my excitement I had almost forgotten about the soapbox I had leapt onto after my birthday, telling all of my friends that Matt would not get the time of day from me anymore. "Well, we just got to talking today, and I *happened* to need directions to this place that *happened* to be near his house...." I gave her the whole story, knowing in my head that I was trying to sell him to her. I did not want her to burst my bubble. Please, I silently pleaded with her, just give him a second chance. I finished telling her all the juicy details and checked her face to gauge her reaction. She opened her mouth and then shut it. She looked hesitant. *Oh no*, I thought, suddenly irritated, *she is not going to share in my excitement.*

"It's really great news, Dani," she said carefully, "but don't forget how hurt you were when he didn't show up to your party. I mean, you shouldn't let him off the hook so easily."

"Oh but I didn't!" I exclaimed. "I forgot to tell you the part where I ripped him a new ass hole for not coming that night. He apologized like a million times." I laughed nervously, wondering if she knew I was lying.

Her expression cleared up a little. "Good! He *should* apologize. What he did was rude and inexcusable. He's an adult and could have called to say he couldn't make it." She must have realized that I looked a little deflated since my arrival and hastily added, "I think it's great, Dani, I really do. I just think you should be a little careful, that's all." She looked at me beseechingly, trying to get me to relent. She was just being protective.

I would be doing the same for her if roles were reversed, I thought begrudgingly. I stared at the paisley pattern on her comforter without responding. Resentment was starting to creep in of its own accord, taking over my giddy jubilation and rising up inside me, threatening to come out of my mouth. I took a breath and tried to shove those feelings deep down inside. *She is not trying to bring me down*, I reminded myself. *She is just looking out for me.*

"I haven't forgotten," I muttered, lying down again on the bed. But I didn't want to remember that night: a night that had been laced with disappointment and embarrassment. I wanted to think about today and the kiss and moving forward.

"Look," she shrugged, "all I'm saying is to go slow…just in case…because if he disappoints you or hurts you again, I'm going to beat his ass." I giggled and she laughed. 'I'm serious, Dani," she said, laughing and flexing a pale, skinny arm. "I'm strong and I will beat him down!"

I rolled off the bed, still laughing and feeling immensely better about the whole situation.

"You tell him that too," she added somewhat sharply, drawing me up short.

I looked at her in surprise; she really had strong reservations about Matt. This may have been the first time we ever disagreed on anything so important.

Elise and I had met at age fourteen: Mr. Smith's homeroom, freshman year of high school. She was shy and somewhat introverted, while I was her polar opposite. Through a mutual friend, we each found out that we were crushing on the same sophomore guy: Adam Miller. Neither one of us had a shot in hell with him, but Elise still wrote me a sweet letter saying that she would much rather be friends with me than feel awkward because we liked the same guy. I agreed and our fledgling friendship was born. As four years of high school went by, we captained winter and spring track together, had many classes together, and eventually became inseparable. In that time, Elise's shyness melted away, and she blossomed into a bigger extrovert than I. By coincidence we ended up attending the same college and became even closer. Our bond was something that I never quite had with anyone else. When Elise was down, I would do anything to make her smile, and when I was hurt, she would dust me off and remind me that I would be fine—and I would believe her. If I ever kept her in the dark about anything, it was only because I did not want her to be disappointed in me. Good girlfriends are hard to come by: ones who will tell you the truth even when it hurts, never be jealous of your accomplishments, and guard your secrets. Elise, always without fail, falls into that category.

As I walked out of her house that night, I was confident I would prove *her* to be overly cautious about the whole thing. *The birthday thing was a fluke*, I scoffed to myself. I would forgive Elise for being so dubious about Matt, I decided as I headed home. Soon she would see that he was anything but the unbecoming picture she had painted in her head after that night; she would see all the wonderful, attractive things that I saw and understand how I could give him a chance.

three

ICE ICE BABY…

"A hospital bed is a parked taxi with the meter running."
—*Groucho Marx*

Okay…okay, make it stop please. Oh God. Oh crap. Try to relax. Come on, come on, I know you can do this. Just hang on. It will be over soon. I bit my lip and felt tears forming and sliding out the corners of my eyes. *Try not to tense against it, they said. Okay, I can do that.* NOT *tense against it.* Except rigid was the only acceptable feeling at the moment. I felt my toes curl so tightly around the stirrups that I thought I might rip them completely independent of the table. *Time to focus on breathing. Hee-hee hoooooo, hee-hee hoooooo. Lamaze breathing does not do shit.* I felt the sweat bead and then drip down from my forehead. It was pooling between my breasts and collecting in the small of my back. I felt hot and cold at the same time. My insides felt liquefied. Grasping the sides of the table, I prayed that it would soon be over. *I cannot believe that I am back here again. When will I get rid of this…this plague on my cervix?*

"Hey, Danielle, can I get you some Advil?" Maria, the nurse, peeked her head in the room, holding two cups and looking at me hesitantly, as if she knew I preferred her to be offering a morphine drip.

"Yes," I gasped out as another particularly violent cramp rocked my abdomen. "Is Dr. B coming back in soon?" I could hear the pathetic pleading in my voice.

"Almost," she said sympathetically as she propped my head up to swallow the two pills. I started to lean up further and she held my shoulders firmly. "Oh no, honey, I'm sorry; the speculum is still in. You can't sit up that much."

I grimaced. How could I forget the fucking speculum was still in? I felt like the goddamn Holland Tunnel. I forced the Advil down as best I could while lying flat on my back with my legs in the air. Feeling a fresh onslaught of tears coming on, I managed to suck them back and put on a wobbly smile for Maria as a thank you for trying to make me feel better.

Maria left, and I started softly singing "Ninety-nine Bottles of Beer on the Wall" to kill time until the Advil began to kick in. I got to sixty-three before I started to feel some relief.

Okay, kiddo, you ready for the next one?"

I nodded silently and put on a fake smile as Dr. Bernstein and Maria came back into the room. Something about him always made me want to seem strong and resilient, even though at this moment I felt like curling into a ball and sobbing. He was an excellent doctor.

"You're a lot tougher than your mother!" he exclaimed, eliciting a weak laugh from me. "She could not have handled this as well as you."

Oh my God, my mother. My mother was in the waiting room, pacing for sure, and working herself into an anxiety attack. That was going to be another performance I would have to put on when I faced her. As long as I acted like the procedure was no big deal, it would save me hours of prodding questions and uncomfortable conversation. Or maybe I could just stick some Xanax in her tea later. I should get an Oscar by the time this day is over.

"Danielle, did you hear me?" Dr B. was looking at me quizzically. "I asked if your boyfriend went to the urologist to get treated for the HPV."

My face flushed red, and I stared at the poster on the wall detailing the correct procedures for destroying medical waste. I considered lying, but there seemed to be no point in lying to my gynecologist. He was not a judgmental friend who would put on an *I told you so* face. His job was to help me, I reminded myself.

"He's not my boyfriend anymore." I felt my face get even hotter, still unable to make eye contact. "And when I told him to go get checked out, he insisted that there was nothing wrong with him." I stared at the floor, wishing with every fiber of my being that I had never met Matt Ryan.

"I see," Dr. B shook his head and muttered something under his breath about being irresponsible.

I felt a tiny surge of something. Relief? Sanity, maybe? This whole time I had been feeling like some kind of dirty, contaminated girl who had gotten what she deserved. But here I was, doing the right thing—as much as it sucked—but taking care of the problem instead of ignoring it. In that second I started to believe that someday, Matt would have to face the consequences as well—probably far into the future and without my knowledge, but I trusted that karmic retribution would find him.

The last time I was here for the cryotherapy, Dr. B froze me twice, but this time my insides were freeze-blasted four times. I wondered why it was different this visit, but then it was time to cringe as the CryoProbe invaded my body again, so all coherent thought had to cease. I tried to picture the CryoProbe as if it were playing a crazy game of Freeze Tag. *Pow! Pow! Pow! You're dead, HPV!* I smiled to myself, then grimaced as the cramps resurfaced.

I sweated through the last two deep freezes, made slightly better by the Advil and the continuous chant in my head of *You can do this. You are tough*, but when it was over and the speculum was finally removed, sitting up was another story. Last time, sitting up had not been an issue, but this visit I had been lying down for a much longer period of time. Quickly sitting up proved to be a bad decision. The room immediately started to spin, and my vision clouded as a nasty headrush took hold of me. Bile surged in my throat, and I gagged.

"Whoa, take it easy! Get up nice and slow. That's it." Dr. B held my arm as I slowly adjusted into a better sitting position. The room stopped whirling around me. "Take your time getting dressed, and I'll tell the girls in the office to schedule you for a follow-up exam before you leave." He started to leave the room so I could put my clothes back on.

"Wait! Dr. B, I have a question. Last time you only froze me twice. Why did we need to do four today?"

Dr. B looked at me seriously, and I felt my stomach clench. He was never serious. Something had to be wrong. I noticed Maria trying to discreetly slip out of the room. *Oh God, what else could happen? I have already lain on a table with my lady business spread for the world to see, with liquid nitrogen being shot up into it. How in the hell could it possibly get any worse?* A year ago I would have told you liquid nitrogen is what they use to make an atomic bomb.

"We had to step things up a notch because last time the cryo-surgery didn't completely dissolve all of the abnormal cells. I decided to freeze you a few more times today so that the LEEP would be the last resort."

"The leap? What is that?" The term *last resort* did not sound very encouraging to me.

"It's spelled L-E-E-P. It stands for Loop Electrosurgical Excision Procedure. It will basically remove the tip of your cervix where all these abnormal cells have congregated, so that they cannot come back."

"Oh." This did not sound good at all. I felt sick to my stomach again. "Does it have to be done in a hospital? Why is it the last resort?" *Please, God, may I never ask you for anything else in my life, don't make me have to go through that electro-whatever. Please. I will go to church. I will do volunteer work. I promise I will* never *have sex again. Well…not with Matt anyway*, I conceded. No point in being totally unrealistic. *But I swear I'll be good! Please, God!*

Dr. B sighed, "We don't like to do the LEEP to someone your age, if possible, because it can potentially—not definitely," he added hastily—"create problems later on during pregnancy." He still had that serious look on his face.

I felt the panic inside me slowly building until I could practically taste it. Was he telling me that I might not be able to have kids? *Is this for real?* I did not want to ask him to clarify; I was terrified of what he might say next. The room was starting to spin again. I reached a shaky hand out to help myself sit and realized I was already sitting.

"And no, you would come here for the procedure, not the hospital. It only takes about twenty-five minutes, but we would administer a local anesthetic beforehand. But let's not think about that yet; we might not even have to go there." He patted my arm and picked up my file. "Be good, kiddo. You'll be fine. I'll talk to you soon."

Gingerly, I walked out to the main desk and handed in my insurance card. That thing was racking up more miles than my Visa. They scheduled me for a checkup six weeks later—six long weeks of wondering if the cryotherapy had worked. *Whoopee*. And *oh boy*, I could not wait to feel like a senior citizen, using Depends again for two weeks. They neglect to tell you until after the procedure that what is frozen must eventually melt, meaning I would now be leaking water while my internal female parts thawed out. As a strong tampon advocate, going back to maxi pads was not high on my list of priorities, but it was what had to be done.

"Oh my God, are you all right? Why are you walking funny? Is she all right? Is everything okay? What did he do?" That was my mother in a nutshell: a barrage of worried questions. Also known to many as the Jewish Inquisition. When I walked into the waiting room, my assumption proved correct. It appeared she had been pacing for the entire time. The carpet actually looked worn. Thank God she did not know that I had already done this once before; then she would really be freaking out. When I received the call from Dr. B telling me we needed to go for round two of cryotherapy, I broke down and told my mother. Well, sort of.

"What do you mean abnormal cells?" she had asked, looking nervous. "What exactly does that mean?" I had purposely used vague terms and employed the use of the word *dysplasia* that I found on WebMD, so she would not automatically associate what I had with sex. It worked like a charm. The words *abnormal* and *precancerous* scared her so much that she did not want any more information. She did, however, want to come with me.

I smiled big for her, to show how fine I was, and told her everything was okay and that I just wanted to go home. Once we were home, I retreated to the living room with my phone, the remote, and a blanket. I could hear my parents speaking in the hallway, their words incomprehensible buzzing. *Great...just what I want to do: have a conversation with my father about my unortho-dox trip to the gynecologist. Yup, sign me up for that one! That will be a father-daughter chat to remember!*

"Hey, Noo, how you doing?" My father strolled into the room, trying to look like he had no idea why I was home at two o'clock in the afternoon on a weekday and looking like shit. Noo was a nickname that spun off of Nanoo, which was derived from Robin Williams's old show *Mork & Mindy*, which our entire fam-ily used to watch on Nick at Nite.

"I'm good, Dad." It was not entirely a lie. Lying on the couch with another dose of Advil in my system was proving to speed my recovery along quite nicely.

"So...they take care of everything for you today?"

There it was: the uncomfortably vague question I had been anticipating. If we were on a sports team together, he would have grunted it without making eye contact, and I would have punched him in the shoulder and nodded. Too bad his "AIDS will kill you and herpes is forever" speech did not cover this particular situation.

"Yup, everything's all good." *Except for the fact that I have to go back in six weeks to make sure everything is all good, then wait a week to hear the good or bad news, and after that maybe get part of my* cervix *chopped off. But yes, I am fine. Could not be better.*

"Glad to hear it." He looked relieved and gave me a hug and a kiss on the forehead.

It is so funny how when you get older you learn how to protect your parents from the things you know they are better off not knowing. Life is just easier for everybody that way. It makes me wonder about all the terrible things that I was completely and blissfully unaware of while growing up.

That afternoon my mom was literally at my beck and call and subjected me to a lot of hugs. In-between that, I watched television and stared out the window, wondering how I was going to keep busy enough for a month and a half to not obsess over whether the cryotherapy had worked. My phone rang, startling me. It was Melissa. Probably calling to see how everything had gone today.

"Hi."

"Hey, I thought you might be sleeping. How are you feeling?"

The concern in her voice made me feel worse. I wanted to tell her I was consumed with dread and stress over what might happen six weeks from now, but I held my tongue. Dr. Olsen always said I had a problem with letting people help me. She told me that my desire to fix things on my own was honorable, but everyone should recognize their limits for when they need to sit back and just admit that they cannot handle everything. Obviously I had not yet been able to overcome that stubborn streak.

"I'm okay. I kind of want to go back to my apartment, but my mother is hovering."

Melissa laughed, knowing exactly how much of a nervous mother I had. "Well that's good, right? If you feel okay to go back to your place? You don't have a roommate to help you, so just make sure you're really feeling all right to be alone for the rest of the night. I'm sure your mom is planning to give you dinner in bed; I don't know if I'd pass that up."

I smiled. She was right. Maybe I *should* just suck it up and stay put for the night. Being alone in my apartment suddenly did not sound all that appealing. Having just moved in, my Internet had not even been hooked up. "Yeah, okay, maybe I'll stay," I said carelessly, as if I were doing everybody else a favor.

"I think you should. Just take it easy and relax tonight. Also," Melissa audibly hesitated, "I wanted to talk to you about something. But first I need you to answer a question, and I need you to answer it honestly. Are you still sleeping with Matt?"

My face felt like it was on fire; I was relieved she could not see it. The answer was *no*. I had not seen him or spoken to him since the day after the Coldplay concert, but he had recently attempted to contact me. Unfortunately, the gutless wimp I had become had actually entertained the idea of returning his call.

"No," I said firmly.

"Do you swear?"

I could hear that no-nonsense tone in her voice, as if she were really saying, *I will find out if you are lying and kick your ass.*

"I swear, I would tell you." *I think I would. If anything had still been happening, she would most likely know about it—eventually, anyway.*

"Okay, well good! I'm proud of you. I know it hasn't been easy, but you need to accept that trying to sleep with him with a relationship no longer in place was not something you could handle. He can handle it because he's a thirty-year-old guy, and he just wants sex. He knows you, it's comfortable, there's no issue for him. But you don't operate that way. You *know* you don't. So I'm really glad to hear that you're not doing that to yourself anymore." She paused. "Are you still there?"

I opened my mouth and then shut it again. I felt stung. The idea of him using me because he was comfortable was always in the back of my head, but hearing it out loud hurt—it hurt a lot. She was right. I did not operate that way, but I tried for a long time because having him occasionally felt better than not having him at all. At least I pretended to believe that. I knew that, underneath it all, I kept hoping that if I hung onto the fringes of our defunct relationship, he would realize what a mistake it had been for us to end it. He just had to.

"Are you mad? I didn't mean to upset you. I think you're being strong and doing a good thing." Her voice cut through my internal jumble of thoughts. "After all, Dani, don't forget what made you tell him it was over in the first place. He wasn't there when you really needed him; that's not easy to forgive. And where has he been through all these doctor visits? He's not an eighteen-year-old kid who gets to panic and ditch his girlfriend because he accidentally gave her gonorrhea. He's a thirty-year-old *man* who's acting like a douchebag."

I laughed. I couldn't argue with any of that. "You didn't upset me," I lied. "I know you're right, and seriously, I'm fine. I know I'm doing the smart thing in staying away from him. Anyway, it's not too hard to stay away from a guy who only calls you for sex when there's an ice age taking place in your pants." Melissa and I both cracked up. My mood started to lift a little. *I will get through this*, I thought with a surge of confidence. *Somehow I will manage.* I had to try to believe that. Otherwise, a Prozac prescription could be in my near future.

I wish I could say that those six weeks flew by and I barely thought about HPV or doctor's visits or Matt, but I would be lying. Matt's text messages took on increased urgency, as if he knew that I had somehow managed to pull away from our sordid situation and was trying to keep me from slipping away completely. I managed to ignore his messages, but I could not bring myself to delete them either. I would lie in bed at night and scroll through them like a true masochist.

As a way to keep myself occupied, I decided to plan a housewarming party in my new apartment. Girls only. I took my time making up an Evite, taking trips to Home Goods to add touches of décor to my place, figuring out snacks to make, and making reservations for us all to have dinner. I scheduled it for the weekend following my appointment with Dr. B, believing that I would be able to celebrate the fact that the second freezing session had worked and I was now free and clear from any more painful procedures. Champagne was even on my list—that is how optimistic I was that the test results would be in my favor.

The Monday before my party, I showed up at Dr. B's office feeling good. It was definitely gone. I was sure of it. When I signed in at the front desk, all the women in the office called out a hello to me. They had gotten to know me quite well over the past year and a half, unfortunately. I knew every single person's name in that office, their husband's names, and even the sex and ages of all their kids. Hopefully, after today, I could finally go back to coming once a year again, and we would no longer know all the intimate details of each other's personal lives.

"Hi, Tina!" I smiled at one of the nurses as she called me in from the waiting room.

"Hey, how are you? What are you here for this time?" She

smiled back. Besides Maria, Tina had been privy to most of my trips here in the past sixteen months.

"Just a pap. It's a follow-up to the cryotherapy I had recently."

"Okay, well good luck. Let's try not to see you around here so much!" She gave me a little wave and went back down the hallway with another patient. A different nurse directed me into room 2, and I hurriedly undressed to put on the paper gown. A few minutes later, Dr. B bustled in with Tina.

"Hello, hello! Long time no see!"

I shook my head and smiled. Throughout this whole thing, having a doctor with his demeanor and sense of humor had really helped. I closed my eyes for a second and silently thanked God for letting me have someone like Dr. B who somehow made this shitty situation seem tolerable.

"Compared to your last few visits, this is a walk in the park, huh?" He and Tina smiled at me.

I laughed and nodded my head. It really was; the exam literally took all of a minute—a far cry from my very first one at age seventeen, when the gynecologist actually reduced me to tears with a regular exam. Those were in the days before Dr. B. I felt like a war veteran. Well, not really, but definitely like I had aged significantly from that first innocent visit more than seven years earlier. Since then, I had been put on birth control, biopsied, and now frozen two times and counting.

"Okay, so call us at the end of the week, and we'll have the results for you." Dr B gathered up my file and handed it to Tina. "Cross your fingers, kiddo. This could be your last visit for a while."

"Let's hope!" I said, faking exasperation. He gave me a quick salute and left me to get dressed. Practically giddy, I threw my clothes back on and decided to go shopping at the mall across the street and buy a new outfit for my party. It was going to be a good week; I could feel it.

"...for pharmacy calls press two, for appointments press three...." Friday had arrived, and I was calling for my test results. Impatiently, I tapped my pen and waited for the right option. Finally! I hit 5 on the dial pad and waited. It rang a few times, and then a machine picked up, "Please leave your name, number and the date of your visit, so a doctor on staff can call you back with your results." *Dammit!* I wanted to talk to a live person. Instead of leaving a message, I hung up. A little deflated, I tried to go back to doing work but could not focus. I tried calling again twenty minutes later—still no answer. After five times of trying over the course of two hours, I finally left a message, hoping that the urgency in my voice would get them to call me back sooner rather than later. I wanted to kick off the weekend with good news.

The day dragged, and every time the phone rang, I answered hoping it was someone from Bergen OB/GYN, and each time I was disappointed. Finally, close to five o'clock, the phone rang, and the caller was whom I had been waiting for all day.

"Hello, Danielle? It's Dr. Bernstein. How are you doing?"

"I'm good! Did you get my test results back? Did the cryotherapy work this time?" I realized I was holding my breath in anticipation. My legs were even shaking a little bit from pent-up anxiety.

"I'm sorry, but the test still came back showing abnormalities," he said soberly. "We're going to have to go ahead and schedule the LEEP. I have an opening during the day on Monday. Can you take off of work? You'll want to go right home afterwards and...." He kept talking, but the ringing in my ears kept me from hearing it. I could not believe that I had been wrong. I was so sure it was over. *Another procedure? A procedure that they had tried to avoid doing because of possible complications to my body afterwards? Could this really be happening?* My mind kept trying to block out what he was saying, while anger welled up inside me. It was so unfair. I wanted to throw something or punch the wall, or run home and hide in my bed. I had been so prepared for good news, I felt like I had been kicked in the face.

Throughout my party the next day, I plastered a fake smile on my face. Nobody seemed to notice that anything was out of the ordinary. We went out for dinner and then came back to drink, watch movies, and play games. It was the ideal girls' night in, but I was in a fog. At one point in the night I just wanted to announce what was going on and thank them for being there to keep me occupied and sane, but I could not do it. I was too embarrassed. Out of the group, I was the "good girl." The only one in the bunch who had slept with just one guy was now going to declare she had an STD? *Way to kill the party*, I thought to myself. *Just keep your mouth shut.* I shuddered, thinking about what I would be going through in a couple of short days. It was best to keep this information to myself. I lay awake that night looking at everyone sprawled out in my apartment, fast asleep. There was not an inch of space left open anywhere, but I felt more alone than I had ever felt in my entire life.

Monday arrived, and my mother picked me up to take me for my LEEP appointment. I was sick to my stomach, too nervous to eat anything. We drove silently the entire way. I am sure she was wondering if *this* would be the visit that would finally fix what was wrong with me. I was right there with her on that sentiment. At the office, I signed in and nodded hello to the women behind the window. They all looked at me with concern, obviously aware that my cryotherapy appointments had been a total bust. Tina came into the waiting room and beckoned for me to follow her. I trudged down the hallway after her into the room that they had done my first biopsy in a year and a half earlier. This room was not like all the others; it had machines that looked very unpleasant and lots of medical tools on a sterile tray. Tina must have seen me looking around uncertainly, because she touched my arm briefly when she handed me the paper robe and said, "Don't worry. They all look a lot scarier than they actually are."

I gave her a faint smile to show I believed her, but after she left the room, I started to feel like I could not breathe. *You are having an anxiety attack*, I told myself sternly. *Just breathe in and out; you do it involuntarily all day long.* Slowly my chest loosened, and my breathing started to come a little more naturally. Then the brisk knock at the door tightened me up again. In walked Dr. B and Tina. They both had this air of seriousness about them, and it really hit me that this was not going to be a visit where I laughed with the two of them about my last vacation or something funny that happened at my office. I felt like I was in attendance at a solemn occasion. It was the death—and autopsy—of the tip of my cervix. For a second I imagined all my organs as people bidding it goodbye and wishing it good luck in the afterlife. I shook my head. All these doctor visits were making me demented.

Dr. B had me lie on the exam table as usual but placed a big blue pad on my thigh, telling me it was to ground the electrical current that he would be using for the procedure. Next he held up the biggest and longest needle I had ever seen and said he would be giving me a local anesthetic in the area where he would be operating so that I would not feel a thing. I squeezed my eyes shut and braced for the pain of the needle. It did not disappoint. I grabbed onto the table as I felt the needle being injected and bit down on my lip until I tasted blood.

"Okay, hard part's done!" he announced while starting to arrange some machines and hook things up that looked very sci-fi to me.

I began to feel a numbness spreading through my midsection and started to relax, knowing that the anesthesia was doing its job. Even after all these visits, my body again bucked against the abnormal feeling of the speculum propping me open. It was still painful. Every time my body tried to relax, the speculum disallowed it; there was no relief. I balked at the thought of succumbing to this feeling for twenty minutes.

I turned my head away as Dr. B started the procedure. At one point I smelled smoke and got dizzy. The entire time, he talked me through it, telling me to keep breathing and stay calm, and that it was almost over. I kept my eyes closed for most of it. There was no pain but a great deal of pressure on my abdomen. I tried to focus on my breathing and ignore the pressure, and just like the cryotherapy, I felt like I was sweating everywhere.

"Just about finished," Dr. B muttered intently, "annnd... okay, we're done." He looked up at me. "You did good, kiddo. Congratulations, it's over."

I smiled with relief and closed my eyes again for a second, to gather my thoughts. My neck was stiff from keeping myself so rigid the whole time. As I opened my eyes again, I turned to the left to straighten the kink out of my neck and ended up facing the medical tray.

"No, don't look at that!" Dr. B called out. "You'll get sick!"

Too late. The contents on the tray were no doubt what he

had just cut out of me, resembling small chunks of bloody flesh. I turned away and heaved. My gag reflex kept coming, and it took about five minutes to get it back under control. *Oh God. I will never get that image out of my head*, I thought disgustedly as another huge wave of nausea washed over me.

"Sorry about that," Dr. B said apologetically as he came and sat on the stool next to the exam table. Tina was moving about the room, cleaning up and labeling things. "A couple of things for us to go over for you now. You may have some bleeding; a little bit is okay, and a lot is not. If there is a lot, call us. No tampons, douches, or baths for the next five weeks. You're going to have a discharge that could last up to four to six weeks, so you'll need to wear a pad. It may or may not have an unpleasant odor. If anything feels wrong to you or you're in pain, do not hesitate to call us." He seemed to be mentally ticking things off, as he made sure to cover everything. "Also, we will schedule you for a follow up in a couple months to make sure all abnormal cells are gone. Don't forget to stop at the desk on your way out and make the appointment." His voice started to take on a more serious tone. "It is *your* job to take care of *your* body," he said. "We send the reminder cards and tell you when you need to be here, but you are the one who needs to get yourself here. Because of that, no woman—I repeat, *no woman*—should *ever* get cervical cancer. It is the one of the most preventable diseases out there, and if you take care of yourself and get yourself here even just once a year, you are doing your part to keep yourself healthy." He sat back, as if drained.

I wondered what it must be like for him when someone came in and he had to tell her she had cervical cancer because she had not been to a doctor in years. It had to be so frustrating. "Don't worry, Dr. B. I always come here when I'm supposed to," I reassured him. I wondered if this was his way of inferring that the LEEP was a serious procedure and should remind me that even if I felt fine, things could be going on in my body that I would never know about otherwise.

"Good. Make sure you always do. Oh, and one more thing: check back with the girls in the office soon. We're going to have a vaccine for HPV available soon; it was approved earlier this year." He wrote *HPV vaccine reminder* on a prescription pad and handed it to me.

My eyes lit up. "A vaccine! Really?" I could barely contain myself. This was the first good news in almost two years of dealing with this shit. "But wait, am I still able to get it? Since I've had it already? Doesn't that put me out of the running?"

"Odds are that you'll still be able to get it, because there are so many strains of HPV. You had one type, this vaccine protects from four different strains, so it will give you protection from the three that you did not contract."

Finally! Something to look forward to! If I was not feeling so sluggish and sick from the LEEP, I might have actually jumped up and down.

Later at home, when the anesthesia had worn off, I gritted my teeth and cradled my stomach as cramps once again reared their ugly head. I wondered if I would be okay to go back to work the following day. More importantly, I wondered what it was going to be like to have some disgusting discharge for four to six weeks. *Ew.* Thank God it was not bathing suit season. Carefully I crawled into bed and lay on my side with my knees drawn up—the only position where the cramping seemed to cease a bit. I stared at the ceiling, exhausted but wide awake. *Is this finally over?* I was afraid to hope for it after the disappointment of the second cryotherapy.

I closed my eyes. *Please God, let this be the last thing I need to go through. Or at least give me the power to handle whatever comes next.* At this point I was afraid that I had used my last vestige of strength. And maybe God had tired of my bargaining.

* * *

I was running—on the track at my high school. My body was tired and my muscles were crying out for me to stop, but something would not let me. I shielded the sun's glare to see who the lone spectator was in the stands watching me. It was Matt. He sat casually with his feet up on the railing. He seemed all of eighteen years old. I kept circling the track, neither of us speaking. Finally, my knees buckled from exhaustion, and I almost fell. I caught myself and walked over to where he was sitting, breathing hard the whole way.

He casually watched me approach. "Hi," he said, looking me up and down.

I nodded back, still unable to catch my breath. "What are you doing here?" I managed to gasp out. He smiled that familiar, wicked smile. I had the urge to run away, but now my feet seemed stuck.

"You want me here," he announced with a smirk. "You're always going to want me here. It's a marathon, baby! And you're the one who signed up!" Then he laughed, loud and hard.

I felt angry and wanted to hit him with my fists, but I could not move my arms. Somehow I just turned and went back to running, while he continued to laugh. I looked down. My clothes were gone except for my underwear. I panicked and started running faster, trying to get away from him, his awful laugh, and his words.

"Everybody knows! Everybody knows!" he screamed. "And they think it's your fault!"

Gasping, I sat up in bed, totally drenched in sweat. I realized I was shaking. Slowly, I leaned back and tried to lie down again and calm my breathing. My cramps were miraculously gone. The rest of the night I could not fall back to sleep and could not stop trembling. I had a sinking feeling that I would be seeing Matt one more time, and I did not know how I would feel when I did…or what I would say. When I peeked out the window the following night and saw him standing outside my apartment, I could not even feign shock when I opened the door.

LET'S TALK ABOUT SEX

"Alcohol is like love. The first kiss is magic, the second is intimate,
the third is routine. After that you take the girl's clothes off."
—*Raymond Chandler*

"**Y**ou've *never* had sex?" Matt was looking at me incredulously, and I was grateful for the darkness in his room. I had not intended to have this conversation in the midst of fooling around. But here we were, with me clad only in a pair of rhinestone-studded, black-lace hipsters and him completely naked. After weeks of making out on office grounds, in each of our cars, and a nearby park, we had finally graduated to a bed—his bed—in his parents' house, trying to be quiet because they were upstairs sleeping. When I arrived an hour earlier, he quietly snuck me into his room, and we immediately started kissing and tearing each other's clothes off. We had gotten down to the last article of clothing—my underwear—when I put my hand on his chest and forced him to sit back.

"I'm not going to have sex with you," I said sternly, while trying to catch my breath. "We haven't even been on a real date yet; you can't expect me to just whip my clothes off and be all about it."

"Okay, sure, sure, no problem," he panted, still reaching for my underwear. "That doesn't mean we can't still have some fun, right?" He gently stuck two fingers inside me, and I could feel my eyes roll back. It felt so good.

"No, no wait," I gasped, trying to wriggle away, "there's something you need to know, ohhh God, that's amazing, don't stop...." I was starting to lose my grasp on why it mattered to say anything at all. He paused for a second, and I steeled myself to make another attempt.

"Don't you want to know why I don't want to have sex with you?" I demanded. "Or do you think that I'll get so caught up that I won't be able to say no?"

Matt sighed, removed his tantalizing hand, then leaned back against his pillows. "Don't worry. I get it," he assured me. "You're just not ready, and it's fine; I'm not at that point yet either. I don't need to have sex tonight. I'm just glad you're here." He pulled me down to this chest and hugged me tight. "I'm just glad you're here," he repeated. "You're...not like anyone else I've dated," he finished awkwardly.

I smiled to myself with my head buried in his chest and snuggled to get closer. I knew what he said was cliché and a little cheesy, but it sounded so sincere. It was crazy how I could never get enough of him. He reached under my chin and drew my face up to kiss me again, and I surrendered to it. My whole body was on fire in an instant. In the back of mind, a little voice was saying, "Go ahead, just do it. When have you ever felt like this?" I shook my head and broke off the kiss.

"I can't have sex with you tonight because I've never had sex before." I said it all in a rush before I once again lost my nerve. There was dead silence. I looked up at him hesitantly. He looked stunned.

"You've never had sex?"

"Never," I confirmed with a nod of my head.

"Never ever? Not even once?" he asked.

"Um, that's kind of the whole idea of never. It means not even once." I smiled faintly, feeling unsure as to how he was taking this news.

"But you're twenty-three! I mean, really?" He leaned back against the pillows but this time went too far and hit his head on the wall with a thud. "Ouch. I just can't believe it..." he rubbed his head, "I mean look at you! You look...and you're twenty-three years old and wow...I mean *wow*."

I sat there, discomfort beginning to set in as I became very much aware of how naked we both were and how he was no longer reaching for me. "Well, okay then," I coughed nervously, "I guess I killed the mood, so I'm just gonna go I think." I began to feel ridiculous for thinking I had to turn it into such a huge announcement. He had said it: I was twenty-three. Maybe he thought I was a deranged freak for waiting so long. Matt was looking completely bewildered, and I was feeling that perhaps it was not a good sign, so I slid off the bed and reached for the lamp.

He grabbed my arm. "No! Don't leave! Why are you leaving?" he said in alarm. "I think it's amazing you're still a virgin. I seriously can't think of a bigger turn-on." He looked at me pleadingly.

"I don't want you to leave, Danielle."

Oh God, he said my name; that was the end of me. I sunk back down on the bed without protest, his hand still grasping my forearm. "Well maybe just a little bit longer," I conceded, just as he suddenly pulled me to his chest again and then flipped over so that I was flat on my back and he was on top of me. The heat and weight of his body was unreal. He was kissing my face, my mouth, my neck, sticking his tongue in my ear until I was writhing beneath him. Just when I was about to throw all caution aside and give him the go-ahead to make love to me all night—as long as he had a condom, of course—he stopped and cradled my face, smoothing the hair off my forehead. I opened my eyes in surprise.

"You really deserve a perfect first time," he whispered, "whether it's with me or somebody else. You waited a long time and you should have it the way you imagined." He sighed. "I would want to give you a perfect night; you should have more than this," he threw a hand back, gesturing at his small, messy room.

I looked at him in shock. While I was spiraling deeper and deeper into having feelings for Matt on more than a crush level, I had wondered where I stood with him. Confidence surged within me. He had to be falling for me just as much as I was falling for him, otherwise he would not care so much about my first time or whether it was "perfect" or not. I pulled my arms from around his shoulders and held his face in my hands to study it.

"What are you doing?" he asked.

"Memorizing you," I whispered, smiling. He smiled back and looked a little embarrassed. I pulled his face down and kissed him with all the passion I was feeling in that moment, hoping he could read my mind. I kissed him with all the feelings that I did not understand but loved at the same time. My mind was made up. I may have been a little bit past my fake deadline of losing my virginity at age eighteen, but I knew with absolute certainty that Matt would be my first lover. Not tonight, but in the near future—the *very* near future, I thought, as our kisses once again grew so intense that I almost believed I would implode from the sensations coursing through my body. My nerve endings were completely inflamed. I felt like a romance novel heroine. No guy before Matt had ever rendered me incapable of thinking clearly; it was the most incredible feeling. He was like a drug—or at least what I imagined a drug to be, since the hardest substance I had ever ingested was aspirin.

The following week we went on our first official date. Everything about the night is emblazoned on my brain. He told me to pick the place, so I chose Hanami, my favorite BYOB Japanese/Chinese restaurant, with excellent sushi and service. (I always get free edamame.) We ate off each other's plates like those gooey couples who usually make me want to puke. We talked long after the bill came and kept talking until the lights dimmed, signaling that the restaurant was getting ready to close. The staff even looked at us apologetically as we walked out, as if they too could see that we were a fledgling couple and hated to disturb us. As I walked over to the passenger side of the car, Matt grabbed my arm and pulled me away from the door. We stood there kissing in the parking lot for several minutes until a Hanami delivery car returning from its last run honked at us, causing us to break apart and smile sheepishly at each other. Once we were in the car, I looked at him, hoping that he did not want to call it a night yet but not knowing what to suggest. He adjusted his mirrors and then looked at me and smiled. "Wanna go get a drink?"

"Of course!" I smiled. I directed him to a neighborhood bar

down the road, and we went in to grab a table in the corner, away from the crowd of Thursday night drinkers. We ordered beers: Amstel Light for him and Yuengling for me.

Back in college my friends used to tease me about my wandering eyes out at the bars. I was always trying to sneak glimpses over the shoulders of a guy I was speaking to just in case I saw someone more interesting or better looking. To this day I'm not sure if I pulled it off successfully or if they had all simply drunk too many Irish Car Bombs to notice—although I can remember a time that I did not pull it off quite as smoothly as I intended. One night at our usual Thursday bar, The Stone Balloon, a decent-looking kid from my political issues class had approached me with a typical, "You're in Begleiter's class on Tuesdays and Thursdays, right?" I had a habit in my college years of entertaining almost anyone who had the balls to come up to me, unless his pickup line was offensive or obnoxious—then it was easy to blow him off. But if a slightly nerdy guy with an overeager expression got up his courage to talk to a girl he did not know, even if I was not attracted, I was always impressed. So this kid—I think his name was Jason—had given it a shot, and I felt I owed him the respect of at least a brief conversation. We introduced ourselves and spoke casually about class and a paper that was due, but about two minutes in, I found myself peeking over his shoulder and trying to think of an excuse to walk away. He had caught me right as I was walking out of the bathroom, and my glass was clearly full, so there went my two polite excuses, shot to hell. Where the fuck were my friends? They always seemed to be on hand and in full twat-swatter mode when I was talking to someone who I actually liked. It figured. And even if I used the drink excuse, he would probably want to accompany me to the bar and pay for it. Unlike most girls, I preferred to pay for things myself. In the professional world there is no such thing as a free lunch, and in college there is no such thing as a free drink. Too many guys felt that you owed them something if they bought you even just a shot at the bar. I was not about to trade my virtue for a two-dollar shot of Popov.

"Danielle, are you listening?"

Shit. No, I wasn't. Somewhat nerdy guy looked faintly annoyed. "Yes! Yes, I was, and I completely agree," I stated emphatically. Always, always, always agree with a guy if you have no idea what he just said, unless he is your husband, boyfriend, or a district attorney.

"You agree with me?" He looked confused.

Uh-oh. Not a good sign.

"I just asked if you had a topic for your final project."

Oh. "Well I meant that I...*agree* that is something that I should be thinking about!" I improvised madly, feeling a bit triumphant. Just then a really good-looking guy from my criminal justice class walked by and smiled at me. I smiled back, wishing criminal justice hottie would rescue me.

"Okay, well you seem busy, so I'll just see you in class." Jason or whatever his name was had taken on a somewhat hostile tone.

I looked back at him, surprised at his sudden abruptness, and then realized he was picking up my lack of interest and was justifiably not thrilled with his deduction. He walked away before I even uttered my own goodbye, and I stood there staring after him, feeling slightly guilty. And for the first time, I wondered why I was always looking for the next best thing. What was I afraid of missing?

I looked across the table at Matt and thought about how I finally knew the answer to that question. For the first time, I was not checking to see who else was in the bar or if there was someone better or hotter. He was my single point of focus, and I was mesmerized. I had been afraid of missing out on someone like him—someone whose voice, words, and…and…*presence* just enveloped me to the point of being completely unaware of anything else. His expressions were so bright when he talked about his family; it was obvious how close he was to his parents and three brothers. His face darkened with disappointment when he explained where he had really wanted to go to college but could not afford tuition and where he had ended up as a result. When I first met him, he had struck me as a fairly private person, so his openness, even if it was due to the wine, beer, or combination of the two, still thrilled me. I interjected with stories of my own, and we sat there talking and laughing for a couple of hours. Not once did my eyes stray from his.

Dates had traditionally been a source of discomfort for me. From the age of fourteen I have been asked out somewhere in the ballpark of a thousand times. For some reason, I always felt as if these guys had preconceived notions about me that were not accurate, but I felt obligated to put on the front that I believed they expected. Every time, without fail, the guy would have a great time and want to see me again—and I knew they would because I would be vastly entertaining and charming at dinner—but I would have a bad taste in my mouth afterwards from not truly being myself and just assumed it would not work, which led to me ducking phone calls until they got the hint. Yeah, I know—I was *that* girl. I suck. But looking back it is clear to me that I just did not know who I really was yet, so it was easier to dish out what I thought each guy wanted, without figuring out what it was that I wanted for myself.

Maybe my little act never transpired because Matt and I began as a casual friendship that, over time, developed so much chemistry before we even had our first date. And maybe I had finally retired it. As we continued to date, there was never even a second where I felt that he was not seeing the real me—even the not-so-attractive side that we all usually try to conceal....

* * *

"You're going to have *such* a good time." I had plastered a huge fake smile on my face. Matt was leaving the next day for a bachelor party. But not a one-nighter in the city or even a two-nighter in Atlantic City; he was going to be spending three nights in the city of sin: Las Vegas. It would be his first trip there...*and* he would be with ten other drunken guys known for bad decision making. Having already been to Vegas twice, I could only imagine what might happen without my knowledge. The thought of it had been keeping me up at night the last week and a half. Combined with the comments some of my male friends had to offer when I was looking for reassurance, I became a walking bundle of paranoia.

"You haven't slept with him yet?" My friend Mark had shaken his head. "You're screwed. He's going to be in *Vegas*, the king of all locations for a bachelor party. He's probably not even going to call until he's in the airport on his way home, hungover as fuck and wanting someone to feel sorry for him."

I bit my lip. *What if Mark is right?* Matt and I were sitting in his car talking and kissing. Mostly kissing. And, of course, the subject of Vegas kept coming up. He had to go home and pack and was asking me about all the good bars and clubs to go to, apparently assuming my two trips there made me some kind of expert. He was so excited to go, and I was trying to share in his enthusiasm, but I was nervous. Although we had become a lot closer, we were not serious yet, and he had not yet called me his girlfriend. I knew I would be so hurt if he did not call me for four whole days. At the time, we talked three or four times a day and always before I went to bed. I did not know what to expect, and an even worse realization hit me as he started talking about how awful work was going to be on Monday since he got back so late on Sunday night.

"Wait a minute…" I was starting to get a terrible sick feeling in my stomach. "I thought you said that your flight came back late afternoon on Sunday?" *Please let what he just said be a mistake,* I thought frantically.

"Well it was," he admitted, "but John, the best man, found a much cheaper flight that has a layover in Chicago going and coming. The downside is that we get back here at about one in the morning, so it's technically Monday." He touched my face just then. "Don't worry, sexy. I'll be in so much withdrawal, I won't even be able to wait until after work to attack you. Make sure you'll be able to have lunch with me." He went to kiss me, but I turned my head.

"Aren't you forgetting something?" I snapped, hating that I sounded like an irritable bitch. Irritable bitches are not attractive. But the bottom had dropped out of my stomach. It was all too new with him; I was not ready to give up the high I received from seeing him every day. I felt selfish. Possessive. It was a foreign feeling.

"What do you mean?" He looked completely puzzled and defensive at my tone.

Yes, he had forgotten. I could not even be that mad at him; with my preoccupation over his trip to Vegas, I had failed to mention my trip for the past couple of weeks. I slid down in the passenger seat and sighed. "Remember my family trip? To Virginia Beach? My whole family is going…" I trailed off, waiting for some spark of recognition on his face. There was none.

He opened his mouth, then shut it. His eyes lit up, and he opened it again. "Yes, I remember!" he exclaimed. "Why, what about it?"

"I leave on Monday at the ass crack of dawn," I said sullenly, wishing that I had never agreed to go on this trip, now seeing eleven days of no Matt stretch out before me like an empty abyss of pure misery. A couple of hours without him felt like torture. Eleven days was just unfathomable. I sunk even lower into my seat. *I trust him, don't I? It will only be a little more than a week. Why am I freaking out?*

"No! You're leaving on Monday? For the whole week? Can't you just not go? Just tell your parents you need to stay here with me," he suggested, grinning. "Seriously though, can you get out of it? I don't want you to go." He had put his hand on my shoulder, and I felt it slip down behind my back and over to my right side so he could get a better grip to pull me over to him.

I finally turned my head away from staring at the windshield to look at him and let him kiss me. The console dug into my stomach, and I tried to hover over it and kiss him at the same time. No good. My muscles were shaking from the effort. I gave up, but rather than break contact, I just let it continue to jab me in the gut. After all, it was nothing compared to the thought of him kissing some other girl in Vegas. My stomach clenched at the thought, and I kissed him with new determination. *Please, God.*

If you have ever cared about me at all, you will keep all the whores and slutty drunk girls away from Matt for the next four days. Amen.

* * *

"We're in Chicago! The next plane leaves in an hour. Miss me yet?"

I held the phone slightly away from my ear. Matt was shouting, and I could hear guys laughing and talking in the background. "Of course! But it sounds like you're having fun," I said as brightly as I could manage.

"What? I'm sorry, I can't hear you!" he yelled.

"Sounds like you're having fun!" I shouted back. My dad came out of the kitchen and gave me a strange look. I probably should not have been sitting in the family room having this conversation, but I had no idea it would turn into a shouting match. I went down the hallway, into my bedroom, shut the door quietly, and turned the volume up on the television. "You sound like you've been drinking!"

"Huh? I'm sorry, sweetie, I just can't hear you with these drunk jackasses yelling every two seconds," he laughed. "We all had some drinks on the plane!" he added. "Anyway, I'm going to go, but I miss you, and you better miss me!"

"I miss you!" I yelled with a huge smile on my face—a real one this time.

Trying to keep busy in an attempt to make time go faster does not have a history of working well for me or any other member of the human race. But trying to keep busy when the guy I have fallen hard for is in Las Vegas at a bachelor party? Nearly impossible. After his call from Chicago around dinnertime, I waited fruitlessly for a late-night text or call from him. I wrote in my journal. Washed some dishes. Picked out my clothes for the next day at work. I watched television until I needed toothpicks to prop my eyes open. *It is the time difference*, I reasoned as I drifted off to sleep. *Mark was wrong; Matt had called from his layover, and he would call from Vegas. He had to call. Please let him call.*

I could not open my eyes yet. The sun's presence was on my lids, announcing the beginning of what would undoubtedly be a slow, monotonous workday. *My alarm must be about to go off*, I thought irritably. The last thing I wanted to do was get up and try to focus at work. All night I had dreamed that I flew out to Las Vegas and had found him kissing other girls in the caves under the waterfalls at the Flamingo hotel pool. *Ugh.* My phone started to ring. My eyes flew open. Seven in the morning here means four in the morning there, and in a city that never goes to bed, it was completely probable that it was him. *Please do not let it be a co-worker telling me they are calling in sick today.* I frantically dug under my sheets and through the pillows, trying to locate my phone. It was Matt!

"Hi!" I answered excitedly, unable to even play it cool and act like he had woken me up.

"Hey! It's so good to hear your voice," he slurred. He was completely hammered, but I did not care.

"You sound a little tipsy," I teased. "Are you having a good time?"

"It's okay," he sounded dismissive. "The girls here just seem so dirty. They try to grab you, and they all look kind of used up. But gambling is good; I'm up two hundred already."

"Girls are trying to grab you?" Me with the one-track mind.

"Don't worry. I push them all away, Danielle, push them

all—" he yawned and became quiet.

"Matt? Did you fall asleep? Matt?" I sat there wondering if I should hang up or try to wake him up. It took me half a second to decide. "Matt, wake up!"

"What? What! I'm here. I'm sorry, I'm so tired. But I wanted to talk to you. Vegas isn't as great as you made it sound," he said sleepily.

"It's not?" I could not believe my luck. "Well, you're just tired from all the flying yesterday. You'll have more fun tonight, I'm sure." I could afford to be generous. After all, he had called me twice, and he had only been gone a day. "Look, I have to get up for work, so you go to sleep and then go hang out at the pool today. I'll be texting you from cubicle hell, okay?" I paused, hoping he hadn't fallen asleep again.

"Okay," he yawned again. "I just have a favor to ask. You need to do something for me."

"Sure, anything!" I went over to my desk to grab a pen and a pad in case he needed me to write something down. He was silent for a full minute. I waited, pen poised over the notepad.

"Can you..." he paused again, "can you not kiss any other guys while I'm gone?"

My mouth dropped open, and the pen fell out of my hand, making a mark on the new white Burba rug in my room. "Why would you think that I would ever even want to kiss anyone other than you?" I faked indignation to show him that it was an unnecessary favor.

"Good! Don't forget," he warned. "That goes for Virginia Beach too...no kissing...."

"No kissing," I promised solemnly. "But...I'm going to book a hotel room."

"Why are you going to book a hotel room?" he sounded confused. Poor kid. Too much alcohol in Vegas had obviously blocked steady blood flow to the brain.

"For when you get back. You live at home, and I live at home. So I'm booking a hotel room, and we're going to finally spend a night together," I stated matter-of-factly.

"Are you serious? That would be amazing. Do it. Definitely do it." He sounded wide awake all of a sudden. "And text me the confirmation number," he added with a smile in his voice.

"You got it, chief!"

"Pal."

"Bud."

"Boss."

"Professor!" I declared.

"Girlfriend," he said after a quick pause.

I hesitated. We always went through this little routine. This was the first time he had ever said *girlfriend*. Was this his way of making it official?

"That's a new one," I offered awkwardly. He laughed. "I like it," I announced quickly, before he could say anything.

"I'm glad," he replied softly, half asleep again. "Have a good day at work."

I pressed end and placed the phone down on my desk thoughtfully. Who would have thought that my…*boyfriend* taking a trip to Vegas would actually enhance the relationship? The world is a strange, strange place. My entire romantic history had been a series of unfortunate events and a source of tragic, comic stories. I was hesitant to trust how easy this all seemed. My track record with the opposite sex left much to be desired.

In elementary school, I was the first girl to have a boyfriend.

It was the third grade, his name was Michael, and one day he showed up at my house with a teddy bear, and that was that: we were going steady. We sat next to each other and held hands during filmstrips, picked each other first in gym class dodgeball, and always partnered up for class projects. He gave me gifts on every holiday and even when he returned from family vacations. I collected a Minnie Mouse ring, more teddy bears than I could count, and beautiful crystal animals that still sit in my parents' curio to this day. In fourth grade we were still going strong. The popular girls in my grade were jealous.

At a birthday party that school year, Keri, one of the ringleaders, announced with a flip of her hair, "Let's have a show of hands. Who thinks that Michael is tired of Danielle and going to dump her?"

I looked up in shock and humiliation. Almost every girl in the room avoided my eyes and raised her hand. My face grew hot, and I knew I might burst into tears any minute.

"Okay," she continued nastily, "who thinks that he won't dump her?"

I slowly raised my hand but kept my gaze down. Everyone started to laugh.

"Don't worry, Danielle," Keri sneered. "He liked me in second grade, you in third grade, so you should have known that it would be someone else in fourth grade."

I ended up calling my mom to pick me up early from that party. I even forgot to get my goody bag. But the girls turned out to be wrong. It was not until fifth grade that Michael "dumped" me.

"Hey, Danielle, I want to talk to you." Michael looked uncomfortable and was fidgeting with the drawstring on his sweatpants. I was getting books out of my locker and stopped to give him my full attention, having no idea what was about to happen. "Okay, well, I really like this girl Hannah in the sixth grade, and I want to ask her out, but I want to let you know that if she turns me down, I'll still go out with you." He looked relieved, as if he had been practicing that very sentence all night and day until he saw me.

I just stood there and stared at him, too shocked to feel anything at first. I was being dumped? Michael was dumping me for a sixth grader? I knew who Hannah was. Dumb blonde…prissy… *sixth grader*! Okay, now I was angry. "So you'll still go out with me if she says no?" I questioned, wanting to make sure I heard him right.

"Oh yes, definitely!" Michael looked like he wanted to hug me for being so understanding.

"So you want me to just *wait around* in case she says no to you?"

"Ummm, well, yeah?" He was starting to see that I was not that understanding.

"Okay…Michael…" I was somewhere in-between yelling and trying not to cry, "are you retarded? I will *not* wait around in case some sixth grader turns you down! I hope she says no to you because then you'll end up all alone!" My chest was heaving, and I slammed my locker shut to stomp away from him down the hall so he would not see me cry. *Please let that blonde slut say no to him,* I thought fiercely.

"Um, Danielle?"

"*What!*" I turned around to find Michael right behind me.

"Well I kind of need the locket back, so I can give it to Hannah if she says yes." He looked terrified and was shifting his weight from one foot to the other.

Several months earlier he had given me a heart-shaped locket for my birthday. My fingers automatically went to my neck in a protective gesture, but by some miracle I had forgotten to put it on that morning. I looked him dead in the eye. "I forgot to wear it today, and you can't have it tomorrow because tonight I'll be flushing it down the toilet." Triumphantly, I turned on my heel and walked away.

"You can't do that!" he called after me.

"Just watch me!" I shouted back. My first foray into the world of dating. It had everything: passion, jealousy, drama. It was no *Gossip Girl*, but then again we were only ten years old. We were not even French kissing yet.

In high school I had a mad crush on a guy who was two years older. All of my friends insisted he was a tool, but I refused to allow their opinion to sway my infatuation. After numerous make-out sessions and lots of talking on the phone, he pulled me into a bathroom at some junior girl's party and fingered me. Still naïve at fifteen, I assumed that meant he wanted to make me his girlfriend. But two days later it was Valentine's Day and I saw him giving another girl a bouquet of red roses. I went into the nearest bathroom and puked up the Domino's pizza and Chipwich I had eaten for lunch. It sucks when your first trip to third base turns out to be a total bust—especially when you realize that your friends were indeed correct. He was such a tool, Ryan Seacrest may have sprang from his loins.

In college I was positive that I had learned my lesson. I was jaded. Wise to the ways of the world. I knew what was up and vowed to always have the upper hand when a guy was interested in me. Then I met Dan. He lived on my floor sophomore year and I originally had the hots for his roommate, Ethan. Dan was just my friend. He came to my room to watch *The Real World*, walked with me to classes, and spent every Thursday with me in the library, catching up on work and studying. By the end of the year, I realized that my feelings for him were way beyond platonic. But it was too late. He was dating a girl who he really liked. Every time I was around him, she was all he talked about, and I would hide my disappointment behind a bright smile. I spent the end of spring semester and the summer kicking myself for not realizing sooner what I could have had with him. I could trace it back to one instant when I should have seized my chance. There had been one night where I was lying on his futon hanging out, and he was on his bottom bunk, his roommate spending the night elsewhere. We were just talking and laughing about nothing in particular, but when he started to fall asleep, I had gotten up to leave. He grabbed my arm.

"Don't leave." He looked at me seriously. "Just stay here and sleep next to me…please?"

I hesitated. What would happen if I stayed? Ruin the friendship, I decided. "I can't, Dan. I want us to stay friends, don't you?" I looked at him, hoping that this conversation would not ruin it either.

He sighed. "Oh all right, just go then." He rolled over and faced the wall.

"Are you mad?"

"No, I'm not mad," was his muffled response.

"Okay, goodnight…" I trailed off, unsure if things would still be okay between us in the morning. I left his room and trudged back to mine, wishing that I wanted to stay. Two months later I realized how much I truly liked him and would have given anything to go back in time and change the course of that night. Stupid, stupid, stupid.

Junior year came and went, and he and I would see each other and make small talk, but we did not have a relationship anything like the previous year. He was still dating the same girl, and I still wondered if I had totally blown it with a really great guy. When senior year rolled around I had finally put the whole notion behind me. This, of course, was when I started running into him with increased frequency.

"Hey, Danielle!"

I turned around to see Dan coming towards me. Thursday night at the Stone Balloon was Mug Night. I had gotten used to seeing Dan here once a week because, with only three bars to choose from at the University of Delaware, this was the only fun place to congregate at on a Thursday night. Tonight something was different though—Dan was extra flirty, buying me drinks and shots and reminiscing about when we first met sophomore year. Both inebriated by the bar's closing time, we stumbled back to my apartment next door. After spending a few obligatory minutes in the living room with my roommates, we hurried to my bedroom. We started kissing, and there was just something so easy and fun about it. We were laughing and kissing, and it felt like I was making out with my very best friend. It was comfortable and delicious at the same time. I was tugging off his shirt when he stopped me for a second.

"I have thought about this for two years," he shook his head. "I can't believe this is finally happening."

I sat back for a minute and looked at him. He had thought about this for two years! What the hell had we been doing for two years? He reached for me again, and I forgot all about wasted time and focused on the present. But when he made a move to undo my jeans, I grabbed his hand.

"I can't," I gasped, so fired up from kissing and touching a guy I had wanted for so long, I could barely breathe.

"Are you still a virgin?" He looked at me hesitantly. I had confided in him sophomore year, and he had never given me a hard time about it—one of the many reasons I liked him so much.

"Yes, but that's not why…" I smiled, a little embarrassed, but hoping he would get my meaning.

He stared hard at me with narrowed eyes for several seconds until recognition set in. "Oh! You have your…okay, I get it," he shrugged and flopped back on the bed and pulled me to his side. "Well that sucks."

I laughed, nestled my head into his shoulder, and ran my fingertips up and down on his chest. No guy I had ever known liked saying the word *period*.

"But next time…" I glanced over at his face to see if I was speaking out of turn, "next time it won't be an issue."

"Next time," he repeated. "Do you know how crazy I was about you sophomore year? But you just wanted to be *friends*," he mocked me.

I leaned up on my elbows so I could look down at his face. "I made a mistake," I admitted. "*But*…when I finally realized how much I liked you, you had a girlfriend, so I couldn't say anything. And last year I barely saw you…." I lay back down and turned my back to him so we could spoon. He brushed the hair off my neck.

"So we both fucked up," he whispered in my ear. It tickled. I shivered and turned back to face him again.

"Yeah we did," I said softly. He pulled me tighter to his chest and, not ten minutes later, he fell asleep. I stayed awake a few minutes longer just to look at him. He was actually here. In my bed. Telling me he had been crazy about me. I snuggled deeper into his chest and smiled to myself. It was going to be a good semester.

"So he was all over me at the bar. He ended up sleeping over last night." It was the next morning and I had rushed over to Elise's apartment to regale her with the details of my unexpected sleepover.

"Oh my God, Dani! This is huge!" She was practically jumping up and down for me. "This is like two-years-in-the-making huge!"

"I know!" I shrieked. Then we completely cracked up.

"Do you think you'd sleep with him?" she asked carefully.

"I do," I said without hesitation. "I mean, does your first time get any better than with a guy you were friends with for so long?"

"I guess not!" she agreed. "How was it when he left this morning?"

I frowned, trying to remember it exactly. Everything that had happened with him had blurred into one big jumble of excitement. "Well I told him my parents were coming today for the weekend and I had to clean up," I said thoughtfully, "and he had a class this afternoon and needed to finish up some reading for it, so he left kind of early I guess." Right then my phone started ringing; it was my roommate, Helen. I showed the phone to Elise. "Helen was awake when we got back last night. She's probably looking for juicy details," I laughed as I flipped the phone open. "Well helloooo, Helen!"

"Hey, Dani," she sounded serious. "Can you come home when you get a chance? I need to talk to you."

My stomach dropped. Something was wrong. "What is it?" I

asked, dread tightening my chest. "Are you okay? Did something happen to your family?"

"No…" she hesitated, "it's about Dan. His girlfriend called here this morning looking for him."

I sat there stunned. *Dan still has a girlfriend? Dan had cheated on his girlfriend with me? Me? The girl he was "crazy about"?* I tasted bile. Elise was waving her hand in my face questioningly, wanting to know what was up.

"Um…I've got to go. Helen needs help with something," I mumbled as I raced out of Elise's apartment, back to my own. Back in my room, I calmed down. *Maybe this girl was his ex-girlfriend and just crazy. Who calls another girl's apartment looking for their boyfriend? That's what cell phones are for!* I was lost in thought when Helen peeked in my room.

"Are you okay?" She sat on the edge of my bed. "I don't know, Dani, I didn't think they were together anymore. She's in my sorority but I mean, I'm not *friends* with the girl, so I just don't know. She said his cell phone was turned off all night and someone told her he had gone home from the bar with you."

I nodded, still not sure what to say about the whole thing. When Dan called, I would ask him to straighten the whole thing out. Except Dan did not call. Not that day or the next day or the day after that. My confusion and hurt gave way to anger—an anger that was at its peak when I finally ran into him two weeks later.

"Are you Danielle?" A vaguely pretty girl with thick makeup, huge boobs, and blonde hair with roots showing was tapping me on the shoulder. I was waiting on line for the bathroom at the Stone Balloon and had no idea who this girl was, nor did I care— that is how bad I had to pee.

"Yes," I answered and swiveled back to face the line of girls creep ever so slowly forward towards the one available stall.

"I'm Dan's girlfriend," I heard her say from behind me.

Uh-oh. Slowly I turned back to face her. I had been so angry at Dan, just waiting for my chance to ream him out, that I completely overlooked the fact that his girlfriend may have been waiting for the same opportunity with me. She started to say something, then burst out crying. I looked around awkwardly. Everyone around us was noticing that a scene was about to erupt. My eyes searched the room desperately for Elise or one of my other friends and ended up locking on Dan across the room. He was leaning against the bar, watching me and his girlfriend and looking like he might shit himself any moment. It gave me a boost of confidence. He was the one who should be worried. The girl was looking down, weeping. I touched her arm.

"Look, I don't chase other girls' boyfriends. You can ask anyone. I seriously didn't know he had a girlfriend. But remember," I looked up to see if Dan was still watching. He was. "Remember that *he* knew he had a girlfriend, and he still came over to my apartment. So if you want to blame someone, you need to take it up with him."

She kept crying, and I started to feel sorry for her. It was so uncomfortable standing there, but I did not know if it was the right time to walk away. After several minutes, I decided that I had no choice since we were not even conversing; I was just awkwardly aware that she had failed to wear waterproof mascara. As I stepped away, her hand shot out and grabbed my arm.

"I will pay you," she whispered urgently. "I'll pay you a thousand dollars to stay away from him. He got me pregnant. Did he tell you that? The piece of shit got me pregnant last year, and I had an abortion. And then he screws you," she broke off into tears again.

I stood there feeling sick over the whole situation. He was not the person I remembered from sophomore year. And this pitiful girl was willing to pay me to stay away from a guy who cheated on her. It was just sad. Sad and grotesque.

"First of all," I said firmly, pulling my arm out of her clenched fingers, "he may be screwing around, but he didn't screw *me*. We just kissed." I started to walk away, and she started to say something else to me, but I interrupted her. "And you can keep your money. It'll be my pleasure to stay away from him," I said in disgust.

Her eyes were welling up again. I pitied her, but I had no desire to be involved in whatever was going on between her and Dan. I had already unknowingly played a part in their sad, twisted little soap opera.

I pushed through the throng of curious people who had gathered to see what was going on and found my way back to the bar and over to my friends. They all looked at me with raised eyebrows. I rolled my eyes and signaled for the bartender to come over so I could order a beer. I took a huge chug and turned back to my friends, ready to fill them in on what happened, when Elise's eyes suddenly grew really wide. She looked completely alarmed. Right then a hand clamped on my shoulder, forcing me to turn around. It was Dan.

"Can I talk to you?" He looked earnest. Pathetic and stupid, but also earnest.

"She has nothing to say to you," Elise retorted from over my shoulder.

I squeezed her hand. "It's okay. Yes, we can talk, Dan." Under

Elise's watchful eye, I escorted him over to the side of the bar near the emergency exit. "So what do you have to say to me?" I stood with my arms crossed over my chest, waiting to hear the line of bullshit he was probably going to spew.

His eyes were darting around and only occasionally settling on mine. "I'm sorry that Laura came over to you," he finally said.. She's my problem, not yours." He stood there looking down and then off to the right.

I waited. "That's it?" I asked incredulously. "That's all you have to say? How about, 'Sorry, Danielle, I didn't mean to lie to you and cheat on my girlfriend with you. I'm sorry she called your apartment fifteen times looking for me. You shouldn't have had to find out that way. I'm sorry I couldn't keep my dick in my pants and had to go home with you!'" I was jabbing him in the chest with my finger, and he was finally looking back at me.

"It's not like we had sex," he scoffed.

I stopped for a minute, stricken by his indifference. *It was not the physical acts we did or did not do; it was what he had said to me. Wasn't it? Did it only count as cheating if we had slept together?* I lost a little bit of my momentum, my inexperience clearly putting me at a disadvantage. "But you said you'd been waiting since sophomore year to be with me. Why would you lie to me?" I was trying to keep the hurt out of my voice and just stay angry.

He shrugged. "I was drunk?" he offered. "I mean, of course I've always been attracted to you, but really, if you think about it…you probably should have *asked* me that night if I had a girlfriend."

Now the anger was back full force. "I should have asked you?" I nearly shouted. "It's not *my* job to ask *you* if you have a girlfriend! It's your job to *remember* you have one and not go home with *me*!"

"Okay, okay, I'm sorry!" He held up his hands in mock surrender. "I admit that I messed up!"

"You didn't admit anything," I lowered my voice, noticing that his frat brothers were practically salivating watching us argue. "You didn't call me; I had no idea what to think. You were my friend, Dan—my good friend. If you want to cheat on your girlfriend, you go find some slutty freshman girl to get you off, not me. Not your *friend* for the last three years." I looked at him and his defensive, guilty expression and tried to reconcile this image with the one I remembered: my friend who made me laugh and who I told my secrets, while he shared his own. They were two different people. Disappointment ran through me at a rampant pace. "Don't ever talk to me again, Dan," I said quietly, then walked away. He made no attempt to stop me, and true to my request, we graduated without ever having another conversation.

My alarm went off, breaking into my reverie. *Matt is not Dan*, I reminded myself, shaking my head to ward off the unpleasant memories. *Matt is the right guy for me.* I could feel it all the way down into my soul—something I had never felt with Dan or any other crush. I was falling in love.

WHEN ONE DOOR CLOSES

"This breakup isn't because I hate you. It's because I love me."
—Mastin Kipp

"What are you doing here?" I stood in the doorway looking at him. My stomach was in knots and still queasy from yesterday's procedure. His expression reminded me of a four-year-old boy whom I used to babysit. It was the face he got right before he did something he knew he would get a timeout for but was determined to do anyway.

"I wanted to see you. Is that so bad?" Matt shifted his weight as if he knew that he had overused that line with me more times than I could possibly count.

"What do you want from me, Matt?" I sighed wearily.

"Nothing! I don't want anything from you." His tone implied that he expected me to be ecstatic that he did not want anything.

Instead I felt like he stabbed me. It was unbelievable how his most casual remark could still hurt me. Dr. Olsen once asked me to sum up in one sentence why I thought Matt and I broke up. After taking two weeks to mull it over, I decided that it was simply because, even when I asked for nothing, he still managed to give me less than that.

"Okay then," I said sarcastically, "if you don't want anything from me, then you don't need to come in." I started to close the door, and he put his hand out to stop me.

"I'm sorry! I love you!"

I paused with the door halfway shut, trying to fight any surge of feeling. He capitalized on my hesitation and gently pushed the door open and stepped inside. We stood in the small nook right inside the doorway and stared at each other. He leaned in to kiss me, and I stepped back.

"Don't," I muttered, turning around and heading into the kitchen. He followed me and leaned against the counter. I kept my back to him and opened the refrigerator.

"Can I get you something to drink?" I asked without looking at him.

"Do you have anything with alcohol?"

I turned around finally. "Alcohol? It's ten o'clock, and it's Tuesday." I could hear how caustic I sounded, but the second he arrived I actually wanted some alcohol myself. "I have beer, wine, and some vodka," I finally offered after he did not immediately answer.

"I'll have a beer as long as you have one too," he said.

I almost laughed out loud. Apparently he thought he was going to get me drunk to have some Tuesday-night booty call the night after I had my insides carved out. Feeling much more sure of myself, I decided to humor him a little bit.

"Sure," I said breezily, "except I think I'll crack into the wine; I'm not in the mood for a beer."

He looked surprised that I agreed so quickly but did not say anything except *thanks* when I handed him a bottle of Yuengling. We stood there at opposite ends of the kitchen, regarding each other silently: me drinking my glass of Pinot Noir and him with his beer. One glass was not enough, and he still was not talking, so I poured myself another. Following my lead he went into the fridge and took another bottle of beer. "So...what?" I finally had to say. His steady gaze was unnerving me, and I was fairly sure he knew it.

"I don't know...how have you been?" he asked.

"Why do you care?" I heard the anger enter my voice. It was just too fresh. He had no idea what I went through yesterday.

"Do you hate me?" He had invoked his typical line of ridiculous questions designed to make me either feel sorry for him or rush to confirm that no, in fact, I did not hate him.

I rolled my eyes and took a sip of wine. "This is stupid," I announced, emboldened by the wine. "What the fuck are we doing?"

He put his beer down and walked over to me. I knew he was going to try to kiss me again. Maybe it was the wine, or that I had been spending so much time lately pretending I was fine when I was really sad and scared, but I knew I would let him. It was an intense kiss. When we finally let go, his expression had totally changed. He no longer looked casual or abashed; he looked determined and resolute.

He grasped my arms tightly. "Let's go to bed," he stated, propelling me towards my bed.

Caught up, I didn't resist until we actually reached the bed. "No! I can't." I looked at Matt, a small part of me still hoping that after all this time I might get the reaction from him that I needed when I told him what I went through yesterday. "I'm not going to have sex with you," I said firmly, "I *can't* have sex with you. Remember back awhile ago…when I was going to the doctor a lot because of what *you* gave me? Well yesterday he had to…he had to do this minor surgical thing and, well, basically…that's why I can't sleep with you." *Medically that is why*, I added silently. I looked at his face, hoping for a flicker of some kind of concern, sympathy, *anything*.

His expression did not change as he continued to maneuver me into my bed. "Whatever you say," he said dismissively.

Disappointment and sadness raced through me, but it was not devastating this time. *He is never going to change*, I thought suddenly. He would always find it easy to say he loved me just as a means to an end. They were just words. They did not mean anything to him. No matter what he said, he would never have some revelation to make him realize how much he wanted to be with me and all of sudden become a more considerate person. I would forever be trying to get him to care about me, and he would always be too involved in his own to notice. High maintenance and exhausting: that was the essence of a relationship with him. Halfheartedly I followed him into my bed.

I did not sleep with him that night, although he tried every which way to con his way into my pajama pants. He finally gave up and rolled over to face the wall and go to sleep, sighing in exasperation. I think I knew it would be the last time I would ever see him. Showing up on a random Tuesday after all this time, willing to stoop and say he loved me to get what he wanted, left me feeling cold. More than anything that night, I needed someone to lie next to me and hold me while I slept, so I let him stay, but I felt empty. I watched him sleep, finally knowing with total certainty that I did not matter to him anymore, and maybe I never really did as much as I would have liked to believe. I was finally ready to accept the truth of the situation.

"You're so careless," I said out loud to his sleeping form. "You're careless with other people's feelings, their emotions…as long as you're getting what you want." I lay awake for a long time staring at the ceiling and listening to him breathe evenly in and out. *The peaceful slumber of someone who always gets his way*, I thought irritably. Eventually, I drifted off to sleep, feeling power-less and lonelier than ever.

The next morning Matt kissed me and announced that he did not want to leave but that he would call me later. I watched him walk towards the door, noting how he could lie so easily to my face and wondering why I had never noticed sooner.

"Wait!" I paused. *Should I do it?* I had nothing left to lose. "I need to know," I hesitated again for a second, "was it ever just me and you? At any point?"

He was completely caught off guard and looked everywhere except at me. "That's not a fair question," he finally said, staring at the floor. "I never asked you that."

I nodded. I had my answer.

"Okay…so I'll call you tonight," he offered, before hastily making his exit.

I did not answer. I had no answer. Not one moment with him had been mine and mine alone.

My mind was a haze that day. I am quite sure I did not ac-complish anything remotely important at work. That night he did not call me. Nor the next night or the night after that. The days started blending together, and I found that I did not care much about anything. I avoided going out, and I was so lost in my own downward spiral that I was ignorant enough to think that nobody noticed. Voicemails were piling up from my friends, but I did not have the energy to return the calls.

His actions and his answer to my question had finally made me accept Matt for what he was, but I could not shake the cloud over me. He had made me feel worthless. I had waited for a genuine relationship only to discover too late that none of it had been real. Officially this left me at rock bottom. And I was no longer seeing Dr. Olsen because my insurance would not cover it. With no idea who to talk to, I began to write. First just angry passages in my journal, then letters to Matt. I had no intention of him ever seeing any of them, but just putting things down on paper would make me feel just a tiny bit better. I would write pages and pages detailing all he had done to hurt me, as well as point out each instance where he had been weak and spineless, a sad excuse for a man, and nothing more than a common liar. Like clockwork, I would shred each letter a few days after writing it, hoping that one day I would not feel the need to write any more of them.

My birthday came a few months later and, once again, I was sharing a beach house with the same girls as the previous year. On my birthday I had way too many shots and ended up vomiting the contents of my stomach, the lining of it, and possibly my small intestine for a day and a half. During my puke fest I received a text message from Matt saying *happy birthday*. It was the first time I had heard from him since the night he showed up at my apartment. At the end of the weekend, I looked again at the text message. He was the last person to send me well wishes on my birthday. I had not written a letter to him in quite awhile but now reached for a pen and began to write one. Except this time, I was determined to mail it.

Dear Matt,

I'm writing to you because I find it utterly ridiculous that you think you can send me a text on my birthday as if we are friends who just haven't spoken lately. I've realized that I'm still angry with you and I've decided to send you this letter so that maybe I can finally say all the things I needed to say a long time ago. So I guess you could say I'm writing this letter more for me than for you, since I don't believe that anything I say or do means anything to you anymore, and possibly never did! Simply put, you're not the person I thought you were. I thought you were the most amazing person I had ever met. You made me feel things I never believed I would be capable of feeling. I waited so long to sleep with a guy who I really cared about, someone who cared just as much about me and wasn't looking for some no-strings-attached bullshit. You knew that and you let me believe that you wanted it too. Instead you kept finding new ways to hurt me, always promising to make it up to me and then, rather than do that, just hurt me all over again in some new twisted fashion. You made me swear to always tell you the truth and never play games, yet you lied constantly. You lied right to my face on so many occasions I can't even name them because this letter would go on forever. You slept with other girls and lied about that too, and therefore let me contract a disease. You gave me HPV and because you are so irresponsible and careless, you will continue to pass it to other unsuspecting girls. You make messes and then run away assuming someone else will clean them up and you'll get away free and clear because of your charm or "feel sorry for me" act. It's pathetic. You are thirty years old and yet you act like a child. You always managed to desert me just when I needed you most, the worst of all being when you let me endure all those doctor and surgical visits on my own. You pretended you had nothing to do with it, and I had to go alone and deal with what you gave me. Do you have any idea what it's like to be told that you're going to have a procedure that could hurt your ability to carry a pregnancy full term? Do you know how terrifying that is even as a small possibility? That is something that I just can't forgive. And I got pretty good at forgiving you for a while there! Because I loved you and I believed that one day you would wake up and stop taking me for granted. But that was never going to happen. You suck people dry and then move on to your next victim. After all that you did, it's impossible for me to even remember you as my first love. And more than anything, I wish I could because then it would be nice to send happy birthday text messages to each other once a year and wish the other one well. But I can only remember you as selfish and weak and berate myself for being too blind to truly see you for so long. I am surrounded by family and friends who care about me and only want the best for me. I feel that you are only surrounded by people just as selfish and spineless as you are, and one day you will find yourself alone as a result. I hope you do something to change that and that you become the person I believed you to be when we first met. Good luck with everything, but I hope that I never see you again.

Danielle

Whoa. But I no longer felt angry. I felt relieved and calm, and I knew it was right to send the letter, which I did the following morning. FedEx. Overnight. Because if you finally find a way to get closure, why not timestamp it for ten o'clock the next morning?

I lost the urge to write any more letters after the day I finally mailed the last one to Matt. And I felt lighter, like I was finally emerging from the dark abyss of depression I had resided in since that night after the LEEP procedure when he had acknowledged that he had never been faithful. In the midst of this enlightenment, I received a card in the mail reminding me that it was time to make an appointment with Dr. Bernstein for a LEEP follow-up. It felt like the final step in leaving Matt behind for good...as long as I got a clean bill of health from Dr. B.

* * *

"Okay, Danielle, we're all done! Nice and quick today. Call us in about four days for results." Dr. B smiled at me as he removed his gloves and threw them in the trash. Maria patted my arm and winked at me.

I was afraid to be too optimistic, but if I got good news in four days, I vowed to spend the whole weekend celebrating down the shore with the girls. My anxiety level was at an all-time high all week, and I was afraid to talk about it for fear of jinxing myself in some way. When Friday arrived, I dialed the doctor's office from work with a shaking hand, pushed in the familiar extension, and waited.

"Hi, Maria! It's Danielle...Sepulveres. Yup, that's why I'm calling...okay, sure, I can hold on." I clenched the receiver and felt my heart going a mile a minute.

"Danielle? You still there?"

"Yes! Yes, I'm here, Maria," I squeaked, shaking uncontrollably now.

"Well the test was all clear."

I could hear the smile in her voice. "All clear? Seriously? You mean I'm fine? No more freezing or cutting or anything?" I realized I was shouting and quickly lowered my voice in case anyone was still in the office.

"That's what it means!" she cheerfully said. "Now I don't want to see your face for a good six to twelve months, okay?" She laughed.

I was elated. "I promise you will *not* see my face there anytime soon! Holy shit, this is so great! Thank you, thank you, thank you!" I was still shaking, sweating now as well.

"You're welcome," she replied, still laughing. "Now go have a good weekend."

"Okay, I will! Thanks, Maria!" I hung up and looked around at my desk. Because of summer hours I could leave in twenty minutes, but I was supposed to take some work with me. I was so scattered I could not even think about what I needed to pack up off my desk. I peeked over the top of my cubicle and made sure everyone else in the office was really out to lunch or gone for the day. "Screw work! My vagina needs to be celebrated! Woohoo!" I yelled. Then I grabbed my keys and ran out the door.

Out at the bar that night, Becky, Jen, and I were debating doing a shot, and I was bursting with my news.

"I'll buy the shot," I announced. "How about a lemon drop or maybe sex on the beach?" I suggested meaningfully. Once everyone agreed and the bartender poured them out, I raised my shot glass and motioned for the girls to do the same.

"Yay for beach house weekends!" Jen called out. She and Becky started to pull their shots back to their mouths.

I quickly yelled out, "And a toast to my vagina!" Then I did my shot and slammed it on the bar.

They were both staring at me. "Your vagina?" Becky asked hesitantly. Then her eyes lit up. "Wait, you mean that you don't have…that thing anymore?"

"HPV." Jen said, nodding. "That's why, right?"

"That's why!" I declared with a huge smile. "I officially got the all-clear from the doctor today!"

"Now we need to find you a new guy!" Jen said excitedly.

I hesitated. I had not thought that far ahead yet. Then I shrugged. "Yeah! Let's find a guy for me to flirt with! And I don't want to see anybody with an empty glass. We are *drinking* tonight!" I yelled.

"Hell yeah!" Becky and Jen yelled in unison.

We spent the rest of the night at Bar A, clinking our beer cans or plastic cups together and sporadically shouting, "To Dani's vagina!" People definitely thought we were nuts, but it was one of the best nights of my life.

The following Monday I felt like a brand new person. No longer damaged or discarded, I was ready to have a whole new attitude about everything. And I was more than ready to start dating again. Or at least I thought I was…until I got a taste of the available dating pool.

"So where in New Jersey do you live?"

I cringed. This guy's voice was so high pitched and girly. I wondered if my mom had confused this dude, and he thought "Dani" was male. I was on the phone with this guy Jared, the nephew of a family friend. We had not met in person yet, but due to my mother's dislike of Matt, she had been trying to get me to call Jared for close to a year. I had finally given in and was regretting my decision immensely, especially when he cracked a joke and proceeded to laugh just like the guy in *Revenge of the Nerds.* Our relationship never made it past some free Verizon minutes after nine o'clock at night.

A few nights later I was out at a local bar and met Eric. He seemed really cute and really nice and asked me for my number before I left. And when he called I actually answered instead of letting it go to voicemail. We went out to dinner a few nights later and were having a fairly fluid conversation until he sat back, tapped his fingers on the table, and declared, "Okay, let's lay it out upfront: what's the story with your ex-boyfriend?"

"What?" I was in the middle of eating one of my ribs (totally not date food, but sometimes I just do not give a shit) and almost spit it out in shock. Who asks about the exes on the first date? Who wants to know *ever*, but really, on the first date? "What do you mean 'what's the story?'" I said slowly.

He laughed. "C'mon, eveeeery girl I know has some sob story about an ex-boyfriend, so let's trade war stories." He leaned forward and grinned at me, and I was suddenly completely ill at ease with him.

"I'm not 'eveeeery girl,'" I responded sharply, "and I have no sob story to share. Sorry, no drama here."

"Wow! That's a first!" He laughed obnoxiously, and I looked around, feeling that he was being a little too loud. "Well I'll share my story then," he offered.

I smiled politely to feign interest, but the checks in the negative column for this guy were rapidly multiplying.

"So I lived with this girl," he began, "but after two years together she cheated on me, so that didn't work out. That was my most recent girlfriend. I was ready to propose to her too," he added thoughtfully, taking a sip of his beer. "Anyway, I lived with this other girl before her, and she cheated on me too, so I think I might be getting a complex!" He slapped his leg and laughed hysterically.

I shifted uncomfortably in my chair and took a big drink of my pinot noir. He seemed to be waiting for some kind of reaction from me, so I frantically tried to think of some other comment, other than, *Sorry for your bad luck. Can I go home now?* I racked my brain. "So you've lived with girlfriends!" I said brightly. "Two of them!"

"Actually three," he corrected me, "but obviously that one didn't work out either, as you can see!" He cackled again.

"Three?" I burst out before I could stop myself. "So they all moved in and out of your house?"

"Oh no," he assured me, "I moved in with them all three times. Do you think you want dessert?"

"What? No, no dessert. So you moved in and out all three times? Where do you live now?" I couldn't stop my line of questioning. The negative column for this guy had spilled over into morbidly fascinating.

"Oh, I live with my parents right now; I've been there for about four weeks, since I broke it off with Kelly—that's the girl I almost proposed to," he reminded me. "You live alone, right? How big is your apartment?"

I stared at him and realized he was not only interviewing for his next girlfriend, but also his next residence. "Check please!" I called out.

The next guy I went out with seemed way more normal right off the bat. His name was Mark, and he did not ask questions about my real estate or laugh like a hyena. He had a job with a financial brokerage firm, which gave us something in common, and he was introduced to me by two of our mutual friends. Everything about him screamed dependable, hardworking, solid... boring. But I did not want to seem picky, so I kept agreeing to see him and would talk to him on the phone most nights. Well, we sort of talked on the phone. He never really had anything to say, unless it was about work or golf. Talking to him was like preheating an oven. Any other topic would barely elicit a response, but then, if work or golf got mentioned, ding! We were at 350 degrees and finally starting to cook. Although I use *cook* loosely. Margin call and birdies do not get me all fired up. I started taking a few days to call him back or developing reasons why I could not hang out, and eventually we went into that relationship limbo that so many semi-couples go into when an essential element is missing. On one of our dates, we went to a Mexican restaurant, and I had a couple of ginormous margaritas, which left me feeling extremely...happy. But at the end of the night, when I still did not want to kiss him, I knew there was no hope. If tequila cannot create chemistry, then the relationship is doomed.

My dating track record was going from bad to worse, regardless of whether I met the guy on my own or we had a third-party introduction. I felt like I was going on dates more for comic material to share with my friends than anything else. But then I met Kyle. We met at a bar about an hour from where I lived, but it turned out that we were both visiting friends and really lived within fifteen minutes of each other. We hit it off pretty well that night and exchanged numbers. Soon we were talking a few nights a week and emailing at a high frequency during the workday, and I found myself thinking about what it would be like to kiss him—something I never did with Mark, Eric, or Jared.

"So I was wondering what you were doing on Thursday after work?" Kyle sounded a little nervous, and I smiled. He probably thought he was in danger of being in the friend zone. It was a Tuesday night, and I was lying in bed talking to him on the phone, waiting for him to ask me out, like I did most nights.

"Thursday?" I feigned confusion. "I don't think anything? Why, what's up?"

"Well there's a new Italian place that opened up near where you live, and I thought we could go grab dinner after work." He paused, and I smiled.

"Sure, works for me," I said happily.

"Awesome. I can make a reservation, but I doubt it will be too crazy during the week," he sounded so relieved.

"Oooh, look at you, making reservations!" I teased. "How fancy are we getting?"

"No! I mean…it's not, um…it's not *that* fancy," he said finally.

"I'm just kidding, Kyle. I can't wait to go," I said softly, feeling guilty that he had gotten so anxious about the whole thing.

"All right, well I'll talk to you tomorrow about it. What time, if you want me to pick you up, and all that stuff." He sounded sure of himself again. "Have a good night, Danielle."

"Goodnight, Kyle." I hung up the phone and rolled over on my side. I could barely sleep the night before I went out with Matt for the first time. I had no doubt that I would sleep well tonight. Maybe it was just the chase with Matt. Knowing that he continually did things to prevent me from ever getting to a real comfort zone had to be what gave it that element of excitement. It was probably better this way. Kyle wants to see me, he asks me out, I say yes, and we go. Matt always seemed more comfortable with telling me he wanted to see me, making other plans, and then drunkenly texting me the whole night saying he could not wait to see me and that he was sorry. How I put up with it I will never know. I used to feel good reading the texts or listening to the voice mails, believing that he cared so much about me. But really…if he cared so much, what was stopping him from just being *with* me instead of saying he wished he were? God, I feel stupid when I think about it. *Reliability could be sexy*, I reasoned. I sighed and tossed to the other side of the bed. I just did not know if I was ready. Ready to get to know someone again and be willing to let him know me. I still could not shake the blow that Matt had delivered to my self-esteem. For once in my life I had let someone *all* the way inside. I let him know every tiny detail, every little nuance of my personality—something I had avoided doing with anyone else. But with Matt, I let him discover me as is—no smoke screens, no act. And he had wanted to walk away. What did that say about me? Dr. Olsen always said that I had to look at it the other way, as in what did that say about him, but I found it hard to be that objective. I only felt that I had finally unveiled myself to someone, and what I had shown was simply not good enough. It is not that easy to bounce back from feeling that way.

* * *

"Do you want dessert?" Kyle pushed the small, leather-bound dessert menu across the table to me. We had been having a good time at dinner, talking and laughing the same way we did on the phone, but for some reason, I felt like my feelings were not strong enough. Not platonic exactly, but somewhere in-between platonic and a crush. And mentally I was cursing myself because I liked everything about him; I just felt like something was missing. But

I obliged him and had dessert, and when he drove me back to my apartment and asked if he could come in, I only hesitated for a second before I agreed.

"So this is it!" I fluttered my hand around nervously. Since my apartment was a studio, there was no grand tour unless you wanted to see the bathroom or the inside of the closet.

"It's really nice," he looked around and then plopped down on the couch and turned on the television. I stood behind the couch, folding and unfolding my hands for a full minute, then walked around and sat on the opposite end. He was the only guy I had been alone with in my apartment other than Matt, and even though I felt so comfortable with Kyle on the phone and at the restaurant, I could not shake the vague uneasy feeling that had come over me. We both stared at the TV, occasionally glancing at each other and smiling quickly before rapidly turning our attention back to the television.

"You can, um, recline back," I cleared my throat, feeling like I had to say something. We were like two totally different people than we were in the restaurant only an hour earlier.

"Oh yeah? The ends recline? I'd rather stretch out." Before I could react, he swung his legs up on the couch and simultaneously reached for my arm and tugged me to lie down. "Oh slick move right there!" he announced.

I giggled. At least we were not sitting like stiff strangers anymore. I nestled against him, feeling my anxiety start to slowly dissipate. He put his chin on my head and wrapped his arms around me. We fell back into silence, but a far more comfortable one. Between the warmth of his body and all the food we ate and wine we drank, I kind of felt myself getting sleepy. I fought to keep my eyes open, but eventually they slipped closed.

* * *

I was getting married. All these faceless people who I did not know were at my house. My dress was beautiful. I stopped one of the faceless girls walking through my house and asked her if she knew who my husband was. She laughed and kissed my face, saying I was the luckiest girl in the world. I desperately tried to find my cell phone to call Elise and have her come over and straighten everything out. I never found it, but Elise still showed up, not in her maid of honor dress but just a sweater and jeans. I saw her walking into the backyard of my house where all the chairs had been set up for the ceremony. I ran towards her.

"I don't know who I'm marrying!" I shouted. "I don't remember saying yes! I'm not ready! How did this happen?"

"Sssshhhh, it's okay," Elise patted my arm. "He's really good looking; everything is going to be fine."

I stood there, chest heaving, wanting to scream and tell everybody that I did not want to get married today.

Elise put a veil on my head and fluffed my dress. "Okay, all set," she said decisively and then took her place at the altar. Suddenly all the seats were filled with the faceless people, Pachelbel's *Canon in D* was playing, and I was walking down the aisle. In mute horror, I looked at all the people as I walked closer to the altar. They were all nodding their faceless heads and whispering about how beautiful I looked. I looked at where the groom should have been standing. He was completely unfamiliar. I was almost all the way to the altar when I took a step and slipped.

* * *

I rocketed into a sitting position and nearly fell off the couch.

"Whoa, are you all right?" Kyle looked alarmed.

It took me a second to pull myself out of the fog of my dream and remember where I was, and with whom. "Oh God, that was so weird," I muttered. "Sorry, I totally fell asleep and had such a bizarre dream."

"Well whatever it was, it wasn't real," he comforted. "Now come lie down again."

I settled back down against him, but something did not feel right. A huge part of me just wanted him to leave so I could be alone. I could not relax, and when he started kissing my neck and face, I became even more rigid, trying to figure out what was wrong with me. I should have been thrilled that a really nice guy was so interested in me, but my usual gut instinct was missing—the one that always gave me the go-ahead. He was getting closer to my mouth, and my window of time to make some sort of decision was rapidly closing. *Oh just do it*, I thought. I turned my head to close the space between our mouths and let him kiss me. It was nice. It was actually pretty good. But his kissing started to take on an urgency, and I felt an alarm go off in my head. I ignored it and kept kissing him back. *Shut up, shut up, shut up*, I fiercely told myself. *You are old enough to sleep with a guy just for the hell of it, to see if you might like him. You do not always have to be in love or think you are falling in love. That is all fairytale nonsense that had not worked out*, I reminded myself. I let him take my shirt off. I did not make a move to take his off like I would have…if it had been Matt, a sneaky, inner voice reminded me. I squeezed my eyes shut tighter and kept kissing Kyle, trying to block out all the memories of being in bed with Matt. All those nights that I had lain with him, my bare skin touching his, wanting time to stand still while I memorized every inch of his body, loving him so much that it hurt. And then my punishment for loving him: frozen insides and turning my cervix into a carving station, along with the persistent worry of what would happen when I got pregnant one day. Kyle had undone his belt and was tugging at my jeans when all of a sudden I snapped.

"No! I can't! I'm sorry, Kyle…I can't. You need to go. You need to *go!*" My voice was nearing hysteria. He was staring at me like I was a mental patient, and I knew I might cry if he did not leave in the next five minutes.

"Um, Danielle…" he started slowly, "what's going on? Why are you freaking out?" His voice had a little bit of an edge to it, and it made me feel even worse. "I mean, you were lying on top of me so…" he raised his eyebrows and shook his head. "I guess I don't get it."

"You think I'm a tease," I said dully. I meant it as a question, but I knew the answer. *I am* not *a tease.* He *had pulled* me *to lie down with him*, I thought angrily.

He sighed and did not answer me.

"You need to leave," I said firmly without looking at him. I picked my shirt up off the floor and put it back on, then straightened the throw pillows. Kyle still sat there, not moving, not saying anything. I felt nauseous. I just wanted to be alone. The thought of someone touching me again the way Matt had was making me sick to my stomach and had my skin crawling. I could not believe what a severe physical reaction I was having, but I knew I needed him out. "Okay, really, please leave," my voice trembled a little this time. I did not understand why he was still sitting on the couch.

Finally, he stood up and started walking to the door. I

watched, knowing that I had overreacted, but not sure now if I should apologize…or explain that I just needed more time. I opened my mouth twice and shut it twice. He turned around when he got to the door, and I opened my mouth for a third time. His face had no expression, and I paused, not sure what to do.

"You're fucked up," he stated blankly.

I stared. He put so much emphasis on *fucked*, it took me aback.

"You're not weird, or cutely neurotic; you are *fucked* in the head," he said slowly and deliberately and then walked out the door.

I stood there staring at the door for several minutes, silently agreeing with him.

six

SEX, LOVE, AND FRED

"So I slowly came to see all of the things that you were made of..."
—*Mary J. Blige*

I called the closest hotel that same day at work after talking to Matt.

"Welcome to the Hilton," a cheery, automated voice proclaimed. "Please press 1 for reservations...." I hit 1 and waited for my promised "reservation specialist."

"Reservation desk," a nasal, male voice answered.

"Hi! I was looking to reserve a room for Saturday, September 11?"

"Saturday, September 11" he repeated. "Okay, our traditional room is $170 for the night. It comes equipped with one king-size bed or two queens. Will that suffice, or would you like to upgrade?"

"That's fine," I asserted, "but I'd like to have one king rather than two queen beds."

"Okay, one…king…bed."

I could hear him clacking away on his keyboard.

"And just to reserve that room, I'm going to need to ask you for a credit card."

As I read off from my Mastercard, my giddiness mounted with each number that I recited.

"You're all set, ma'am. Can I do anything else for you?"

"No, thank you! That's all!" I could barely contain my excitement.

"Well you enjoy your stay at the Pearl River Hilton on September 11, 2004, and here is your confirmation number…."

I wrote down the twelve-digit number and then carefully transposed it into my cell phone and sent it as a text message to Matt. I wrote, *Hope u r ready for Saturday, September 11! Just remember 1YTJ26172PY6.* A few minutes later he wrote back, *Is that what I think it is???* I responded with, *You bet ur ass!*

Ugh. I turned my attention back to work. Now I just had to make it to September 11! Matt would be coming back from Las Vegas in a couple of days, but I still had to make it through a week of vacation with my family. *Shit. Maybe I should have made it sooner, like the Saturday after getting back from Virginia.* I wondered how many people knew so far in advance the exact day they would lose their virginity. I had always wished it would happen more spontaneously. But how could I complain when I had waited long enough and was falling more and more for Matt every day. It was really pretty ideal when all was said and done.

The week away in Virginia went slower than an ant trying to scale Everest. I talked to Matt several times a day, but it was the worst at night.

"I wish you were here!" he sounded frustrated. "My parents are away, and you could sleep over, and it's driving me nuts that you're gone until Sunday!"

"It's not easy for me either!" I protested. "I feel like I haven't seen you in so long. I got very used to seeing you every day!"

"Just hurry up and get here, okay? Maybe you can come home a day earlier?" he asked hopefully.

I shook my head. "Definitely not going to happen. My parents don't get much vacation time, and there is no way that they are leaving early."

"It was worth a shot," he sighed. "How much do you miss me?" he asked suggestively.

"Just wait until I get home," I whispered, "and you'll *see* how much I missed you."

"Oh really? What are you going to do to me?" His tone had gotten lower and even sexier.

I lowered my voice because family members were in and out of the room, and I was positive they were eavesdropping. "I can't really discuss that with you right now," I said stiffly as my dad poked his head in the room to say goodnight.

Matt started laughing. "Yeah I guess you can't really talk dirty with your parents in the next room." he remarked good-naturedly, while I kept my hand over the phone and waved and mouthed goodnight to my dad. My dad left, and I relaxed.

"Sorry about that," I sighed. "There's not much privacy here. But for the record, you don't even know how much I miss you and want to see you. What are you doing on Sunday? Can I see you when I get home?"

"What time are you getting home?" he asked. "I have an engagement party, but it shouldn't run too late. It's forty minutes away though. We'll have to work something out."

"Please don't tell me I have to wait until Monday to see you!" I cried. "Then I have to sit through an entire workday and settle for emailing you until I get to see you after work. I *need* to see you on Sunday!" I leaned back against the pillows on the bed in mute frustration.

Family trips always had the worst timing for me, even dating back to high school. One of my crushes had invited me to meet him at the traditional bonfire the night before Thanksgiving, but my parents said we had to leave that night for my grandmother's house so we could beat traffic. I remember passing the high school on the way to the highway and seeing the bonfire lighting up the sky. Pressing my head against the glass, I tried to see if I could make out any of the people milling about in the school parking lot. Frustration racked my brain, and I wondered if my crush was thinking I stood him up. Back at school after Thanksgiving weekend, my crush was seen walking through the hallway holding hands with a freshman girl. Everyone said they hooked up at the bonfire and started going out over the weekend. I guess he could not have been too upset that I had not shown.

On the way back from Virginia, the eye of a hurricane swept through Delaware as we were on I-95. The rain poured so hard and for so long, we had to pull off the highway and wait it out. I was ridiculously antsy. I was so close yet still so far from being home. Matt was not leaving for the engagement party for a few more hours, and I was hoping to catch him before he did. But the rain was throwing a huge wrench into my plans. Finally we were safely able to get on the road again, but it was still slow going. There were floods, accidents—a full-blown Murphy's Law kind of a day. Normally coming home from Delaware takes two and a half hours. This time it took almost five. It was almost nine o'clock at night when we pulled into the driveway. Then we had to unload the car. I dejectedly helped carry packages into the house, then sat down in my room to text Matt. *Have fun at the party. Just got home, going to bed.* He wrote back right away, *Glad u r finally home! C u tomorrow* J

The next day back at work did not drag as badly as I had feared, mostly due to the ridiculous amount of work that had piled up in my absence. And Matt and I snuck away in the middle of the day to meet in stairwell A, our little, secret, midday rendez-vous spot. The building was so big, no one ever took the stairs, so we were guaranteed privacy to meet and make out for a few minutes. I reasoned that, since smokers were able to take smoke breaks, and I was not a smoker, I should be allowed a kissing break. I probably took the same amount of time as a smoker— and what I was doing was healthier! It was so hard to tear myself away from him and go back to the office before anyone noticed how long I had been gone.

"I'll see you after work?" I asked breathlessly, in-between kissing him.

"Mmmhmmm," he replied, pushing me back against the stairwell wall and not letting me escape. I tugged on his tie and threw my arms back around his neck, figuring I could spare another minute or two.

Many minutes later, I was back at my desk, still heady from kissing him for so long. Our chemistry was so intense; I could barely stand it. *When would September 11 get here?* Later in the day, after the gym, I went and sat with him in his car for a few minutes before heading home. I touched his face.

"I missed you so much," I admitted softly.

He looked at me seriously. "I missed you too." He pulled my face closer and kissed me. "Don't ever leave me for that long again," he muttered and started kissing my neck and my ear.

"Don't you think it's crazy though?" I gasped as he hit a really sensitive spot on my neck. "I mean, really, it was only a week. But it felt *so* long."

He stopped kissing my neck and looked me right in the eye. "One day is too long," he said seriously.

I felt my heart lurch, but I did not know what to say, so I just kissed him. And kissed him and kissed him and kissed him.

A few days later, Elise called and wanted to make plans to go out in the city on the upcoming Saturday night. "Invite Matt," she offered. "I don't think Jack can make it out, but I really want to meet Matt."

"Are you sure?" I asked. "I can come myself, and we can do a girls' night if you'd rather?"

"No, invite him! Let's see who else is around that night too. We'll go somewhere really fun." She seemed excited to meet him, totally different from when I first told her about my clandestine tryst with him in the rain. I knew I had to take advantage of the situation. I called Matt immediately.

"Saturday?" he said hesitantly. "I had told my brother CJ I would hang out with him, since he's leaving in a few days for California for work."

"Well why not just invite him?" I asked. "There's going to be a bunch of people going out that night. Maybe he'll flirt with one of my girlfriends!"

Matt laughed. "Okay, that sounds great," he agreed. "We'll all head into the city on Saturday."

"Plus we can crash at Elise's apartment," I added, "so everybody can drink!"

"Even better!" he exclaimed. "We'll talk about it more as it gets closer, but there's enough room at Elise's for you, me, and my brother to crash?"

"Oh yeah," I said breezily, "she said it's no problem, plus her roommate hasn't moved in yet, so there's a completely empty bedroom and a pullout sofa in the living room."

"Awesome. CJ and I will go get a bunch of alcohol for pregaming," he promised.

"Great! Elise will definitely appreciate guests who arrive with alcohol!" I laughed. "We'll talk about it more on Friday."

Plans for Saturday shaped up throughout the rest of the week, and it seemed like a nice-sized group of people were meeting up that night. I was thrilled to be able to finally introduce Matt to some of my friends. Elise, Matt, CJ, and I headed into the city together to pregame at Elise's apartment before meeting up with some other friends at The Pioneer Bar. We played a few drinking games, and by the time we left her apartment, we were all pretty buzzed. The night flew by; we were all having a great time. Different people kept buying rounds of shots. I was exhilarated, drunk, and happy. Elise and I danced like crazy. Matt never left my side. It was so much fun, and I was feeling like Matt and I were officially a couple.

It got later, and people started to separate and head to different bars or home. Our original four got in a cab and headed to another bar closer to Elise's apartment. We had one more drink there and then decided it was time for food and bed. Matt held my hand as we walked the few blocks from the bar to the apartment. CJ was in front of us, chowing down on an enormous cheesesteak, and Elise was even further ahead, on the phone with Jack.

"I had fun tonight," Matt looked at me and squeezed my hand tightly.

I looked up at him and smiled. "Me too. I had a great time tonight," I squeezed back. I yawned. "I'm sleepy," I announced.

"Don't get too sleepy," he leaned down and whispered in my ear.

I shivered, suddenly wide awake and aroused.

Since we had lagged behind, Elise and CJ were already in the apartment when we got back. Elise was brushing her teeth, and CJ was passed out on the couch. We looked at him, then looked at each other.

"Let's not wake him up," I said, hoping Matt would say that we should. CJ should have been sleeping in the other room so Matt and I could share the pull-out couch.

"Well, we'll take the other room, right?" he asked. "That's better anyway; it's empty and it has a door," he added meaningfully.

I hesitated. We would have to sleep on the floor. "I guess so." I knew I sounded unconvinced. But at least I had brought in the huge comforter that was always in the trunk of my car. It was king size, so maybe it was big enough to lie on and wrap over us. Matt went into the other bedroom, and I hugged Elise goodnight.

"Be good," she warned with a smile as she shut her bedroom door. I winked at her, then picked up the comforter and carried it into the other room. Matt had changed into shorts and a sleeveless shirt. I undressed and put on shorts and a tank top. He watched me.

"I don't know why you're putting clothes *on*," he feigned confusion.

I giggled. "You need something to take off! Otherwise, where is the fun?" I informed him saucily.

"Get over here," he demanded. "Right. *Now*."

I obliged by lying down next to him. I ran my hands over his shoulders and back and finally wrapped them around his neck. We started to kiss. And then clothes started to come off. And then there were no clothes at all. I definitely wanted more, but I had to stop it. I pushed on his chest and turned my face away.

"What's the matter?" he panted. "Do you not want to? Are you not ready?"

"No, I am!" I swore. "But we need a condom. Do you have one?"

He threw his head back. "Shit. *Shit*. I don't think I do. I'm sorry." He laid his head on my chest, and I kissed the top of it. "I didn't think this would happen tonight, since we planned on the night at the Hilton and all, so I didn't bother bringing anything."

Ironically, I felt kind of pleased that he had not assumed that he was going to get to sleep with me tonight. "Shhhh, it's okay," I assured him. "It'll happen soon enough. I'm actually kind of impressed that you didn't assume you'd get sex tonight," I added.

"I didn't assume that I'd *make love* to you tonight," he corrected. "I wanted you to have your night in a hotel, not crashing in your friend's apartment. But I got a little carried away. I'm sorry." He looked at me sheepishly. "Forgive me?"

"Forgive you for what?" I asked. "I wanted to as much as you. And if you had protection on you, we would not be talking right now!" We laughed.

"We'd be doing a different kind of talking," he grinned wickedly. "I'm going to run to the bathroom. I'll be right back."

I watched him leave and pulled part of the comforter back around me. It was sort of unnerving that there were no curtains in this room and that we were in plain view of several apartments. Hopefully everyone was sleeping and not watching the Matt and Danielle "will they or won't they" show. A minute later, Matt came back into the room. After he carefully shut the door, he stood there, not moving. He had a strange expression on his face.

I sat up. "Everything okay?" I said, worried he was going to tell me CJ was puking in the other room. Elise would kill me.

He took a step forward and kneeled down to my level. "I found something," he said solemnly.

"Found something?" I repeated, confused.

He opened his hand and out fell three Trojan condoms.

I stared at them for a second and then looked at him. "Where did you find these?" I asked, knowing that Elise would definitely not mind, as long as I replaced them.

Matt laughed. "CJ's wallet!" he whispered loudly.

I cracked up. "I guess he thought he'd be getting a lot of lovin' tonight," I joked, suddenly feeling nervous. Realizing that our one last barrier was out of the way, I felt a drop in the pit of my stomach that must have shown on my face.

Matt brushed my hair back. "We don't have to do this tonight. This is all your decision," he said seriously.

I shook my head. "I want to," I said determinedly.

"You're sure?" he asked.

"Positive," I stated.

We started kissing again. It felt different than all my other kisses with him—maybe because I did not have to think about when to pull the brakes or worry whether I was making a bad decision. There were no brakes, and the decisions were made. It was not long before he had me going crazy beneath him and wanting that one thing that I had wanted for such a long time from someone like him.

"You okay?" he breathed. I nodded and arched my back, craving more closeness with him, unable to speak. "You are so beautiful," he whispered. "I wanted you the first day you said hello to me. I can't believe that I'm here with you right now. I've wanted this for a long time."

"I wanted you too," I whispered. "Matt, whatever you do?"

"Yeah?"

"Just don't stop," I moaned.

He handed me the condom, and after two tries I got the stupid thing open. It was lubricated, so it was slippery, and getting it on his penis took some persistence on my part. He slowly started to go inside me.

"Holy shit, you are so tight," he whispered. "You are so fucking tight. I love it." He started moving in and out, and I moved with him, mimicking his motions. It felt good, but it also hurt. "Does it hurt?" he asked. "Are you okay?"

I nodded. "I'm okay. But it hurts a little bit," I admitted.

He stopped and pulled out. "Let's try something else," he suggested. He lay on his back and pulled me on top of him. I guided him back inside me and suddenly felt like I was choking. It felt like his penis was in my throat. "Is this better?" he asked.

I tried to nod but could not even lie. I shook my head. We went back to him on top of me and then tried a few other positions. All were better than me on top but slightly uncomfortable. We ended up using two of the three condoms that night. Hours went by before we actually went to sleep.

I woke up the next morning before Matt did, and I was more sore than I had ever been in my entire life. Quietly, I snuck out of the room, tiptoed past CJ, and crept into Elise's room. I crawled into her bed and she semi-woke up.

"Hey," she said sleepily. "Everything all right?"

"Everything is fine," I assured her.

She had one eye open, but it was enough to see that I was wide awake. She slowly opened the other eye and stared at me. "Did you…?" she started to question, and I began to turn red. "You did! I knew you would! I saw how the two of you were all night. I totally called it." She sat up and smacked my arm. "How was it?"

"It was good! But it kind of hurt, which I expected. I'm sure it will start to feel even better next time, right?"

"Definitely will," she nodded.

"And there was another thing," I paused and felt my face turn even redder. "You know when you're on top? It kind of feels like… it's sort of like—"

"Like it's in your throat?" Elise supplied.

"Yes! Exactly! What *is* that?" I laughed, happy she understood.

"That goes away too. Don't worry about it," she said dismissively. "It happened to me too the first time; I felt like if I opened my mouth a penis might pop out of it."

I laughed harder. That was exactly what it had felt like. "Okay, well I'm going to go back before he wakes up," I whispered. "See you when we get up for real in an hour or two."

She yawned and smiled. "Morning sex is nice," I heard her say all muffled from underneath her comforter.

"I'll remember that," I promised. I slipped back through the living room and into the other bedroom. Matt woke up when I opened the door.

"Hey, where did you go?" he grumbled.

"Um, I went to talk to Elise," I admitted.

He smiled. "Does she approve?" he asked wryly.

"What are you talking about?" I faked a puzzled look, then smiled. "Of course she does. Now kiss me, because I hear that morning sex is pretty good."

He looked surprised, then smiled. "So you're ready for round three?" He reached for me and pulled me down to his chest. "You asked for it!" he growled and started kissing my neck and licking my ear.

"Sssshhhh, not so loud," I admonished, but I really did not care. I just never wanted him to stop touching me.

We emerged from the room a couple of hours later to find CJ and Elise waiting patiently in the living room, watching television.

"Can we go now?" CJ asked crankily. "I'm starving!"

I glanced at Elise, and she rolled her eyes—definitely a sign that she was not a member of the CJ Fan Club. I did not get a good taste of his personality the night before because I had been so involved with Matt, but I assumed there would be plenty of time to get to know him better. I drove the two of them home to Suffern without much conversation. Matt and I would occasionally look at each other and smile a small, secretive smile. When we pulled up in front of their house, CJ jumped out of the car with a quick *thanks* and took off into the house. I looked at Matt, suddenly shy. I felt like a different person. Branded. Totally belonging to him.

"So…you'll call me later?" I asked him, wishing that at least one of us had our own apartment.

He leaned in and kissed me. "Of course! I had a really good time with you last night, so thank you again."

"You don't have to *thank* me. And I always have a good time with you." I touched his face and leaned in to kiss him one more time. Leaving him was my absolute least favorite thing to do.

"You're not around for Labor Day weekend, right?" he asked suddenly.

I shook my head. "No, it's my grandmother's birthday weekend, so I'll be down in Toms River." I touched his hand.

"I really want to see you this week before the long weekend, in case we don't get to hang out, okay?" he looked at me imploringly.

"Definitely!" I loved that he was trying to make plans in advance. It made me so happy. We kissed one more time, and then he reluctantly opened the door and got out of the car. I watched him walk to his front door and blew him a kiss when he turned around. He smiled and pretended to catch it.

* * *

"Hi! I'm Mike! A friend of Matt and CJ!"

"Hi, Mike!" I shouted, "I'm Danielle, Matt's girlfriend!" I was out with Matt at a bar in Nyack, aptly named Zoo Bar. CJ was also there, along with some other guys who were friends of both brothers. I had driven to Matt's house, and we were planning on staying in when CJ called and coerced us to meet him out. I drove us over there so I could force Matt's hand to leave when I was ready. So I passed on all the rounds of shots that these guys were consuming and spent time nursing a couple of beers.

"So, Danielle, how did you and my brother meet?" CJ had plopped himself on a bar stool in front of me.

I was startled. He had not really made any effort to get to know me prior, even though I had become a regular fixture at his house. This was totally out of character from what I knew of him so far. "Well we work in the same building and go to the same gym, so we saw each other so often—"

"Okay, that's cool," he interrupted and waved the bartender over to order another drink.

"Okayyyy," I muttered. So much for having any kind of a relationship with the brother.

Matt walked by then and saw us sitting together. "Hey, are you guys bonding?" he kidded. "Are you talking about all my good qualities?"

I smiled at him and opened my mouth, but CJ beat me to it.

"She's like my sister already!" he proclaimed.

I looked at him in shock. Nothing could be further than the truth.

"We were just about to hug," he added. He reached for me so fast, I almost toppled off my stool. Before I knew it, he had me in a full embrace. Over his shoulder, I saw Matt smiling, and I smiled back until CJ started whispering in my ear, "Look, I don't like you."

I stiffened and tried to pull away from him, but he clung on tightly.

"I don't trust you," he added. "And if you do anything to hurt my brother, I will burn your house down and do terrible things to your family. Got it?" He let go then, and I stumbled back.

Matt walked closer and said, "That was sweet," then turned to CJ and added, "but next time, don't touch my girl so much."

I was shaking, and CJ gave me a warning look. "Umm, Matt," I mumbled, "can we go? I don't feel so well…."

"What's wrong?" he looked at me with concern. "What happened?"

"Nothing, I just think I really want to go, if that's okay."

CJ walked away, and Matt looked at me hard. "Did he say something to you?" he asked carefully. "You should know that he's never serious; he just gets jealous when I'm not hanging out with him as much as I usually do. Did he try to make you feel bad about spending so much time with me?"

I shook my head and smiled. "I don't know what you're talking about. I just want to go home, okay?" I tugged on his arm. "Please?"

"Sure," he looked perturbed, as if he knew I was not telling him the truth, but obligingly followed me out the door, and we drove back to his house. I was torn about telling him what CJ had said, but if it was really just petty jealousy, I could handle it, I reasoned silently. The malevolence in his words, however, made me uneasy. After all, who threatens to burn someone's house down? Everyone has crazy family members, but this felt a little bit beyond regular crazy—like sociopath crazy.

Our lovemaking had gotten better and better for me over the last couple of weeks. My need for him was overwhelming and unlike anything I had ever experienced. I could never get enough, and some nights we made love for hours until I had to call home and make up some excuse for where I was spending the night, mostly because I was too spent to move. We always joked that I was trying to make up for lost time. For two people who both lived under their parents' roofs, we managed to have sex quite often, sometimes every day of the week, with "marathon sessions"—as we liked to refer to them—on the weekends.

One night in November, we had gone out to dinner and were back at his house in his bed. We were in the midst of kissing when he stopped and quickly mumbled, "I love you."

My eyes flew open. We had drunk a lot of wine at dinner, and

I was not sure if I was imagining things. "*What* did you say?" I asked.

"I said I want you," he uttered quickly and then tried to kiss me again.

"No, you didn't. You said something else." I looked at him hard. "Say it again."

"I want you," he obliged.

"No! That's not what you said." I gazed up at him, disappointed. He tried to kiss me again, but I turned my face. "It's fine," I said softly, "but I want *you* to know that I love you more than anything." I stole a peek at him. He looked stunned. "I would do anything for you. You make me happier than I've ever been in my entire life."

"You really mean that?" he asked seriously.

"With my whole heart," I said solemnly.

He closed his eyes. "I don't deserve you," he muttered. "You're not like anyone I've ever been with. You make me feel like I'm this wonderful, amazing person, and half the time I wonder when you're going to realize that I'm not…that I'm not perfect."

I stared at him in disbelief. "I don't think you're perfect. I love you *because* you're *not* perfect. I love you because just seeing you makes me happy. Just hearing your voice makes me fall in love with you all over again. I love you because you make *me* feel like this wonderful, amazing person, and sometimes *I* wonder when you'll wake up and think you made a mistake! I just…love you. It just is…it's that simple," I said quietly. "If you don't want that from me, now would be a good time to tell me." I turned on my side. I couldn't believe we were saying *I love you* for the first time, and I was simultaneously bringing up the possibility of us breaking up—all while we were naked in bed. What a perfect scenario.

"No, I do want it. I just want to be able to give you everything you want and deserve," he insisted. "You deserve so much, and sometimes I feel like I'm falling short of that."

"If you were falling short, I wouldn't be here, Matt," I firmly told him.

He sighed and then snuggled up next to me to spoon. "I love you, Danielle."

"I love you back," I smiled. I felt perfectly content cuddled up next to him. We belonged to each other.

A few weeks later, the day before Thanksgiving, we were on the phone at work discussing our next hotel "night out."

"We could go back to the Hilton," I was musing, "but what about that party I'm supposed to go to in Hoboken soon. Why don't you go with me to that, and we'll stay at that Sheraton in Weehawken?"

"That could work too," he conceded. "Sheratons have the Sweet Sleeper bed that I love." We both laughed.

"Oh wait! I'm so stupid! I totally forgot! Our family friends own a motel right near the Binghamton on River Road! Let's stay there. My friend Fred is the manager, and he'll probably get us one of the good rooms for a discounted rate. I'll call him and ask him."

"Hey, if there's a connection we can use, let's do it," he agreed. "By the way, what are you doing tonight?"

I grimaced. The night before Thanksgiving always felt like amateur night; the bars were too crowded and stupid dive bars had ridiculous cover charges to even enter. "I don't know. The night before Thanksgiving is so crowded everywhere. Are you supposed to meet up with high school friends or something?"

"Yeah, I think a bunch of people are going to Zoo Bar in

Nyack. Why don't you come there with me?"

"Okay, maybe. I have to see what my friends are doing," I reminded him. "Now let me go do work so I can get out of here early today, okay punk?"

"Later punk. Call me when you leave!"

We both hung up. Rather than do work, I called my father to see if he had Fred's work number. He did not and suggested I try Fred's cell. Every time I picked up the phone to dial Fred, another line rang and I got sidetracked. After three tries, I finally picked up the phone to call Fred, and again another line rang. Annoyed, I answered it.

"Hi, this is Danielle."

"Dani? Did you try to call Fred?" It was my dad.

"Well I was just about to—"

"Don't," my dad said sharply. "Don't call him."

"Okay…" I said perplexed. "Why?"

My dad was silent for a full minute. "I wouldn't have told you this while you're at work," he started slowly, "but since you were about to call him and I just found out…I figured I had to call you back and tell you myself."

"Tell me what?" I was completely confused.

"Fred passed away this morning," he said simply.

I almost dropped the phone. "He what? He what? He what? What are you talking about?" I realized I was shrieking into the phone, and my whole office had gone silent.

"Ssshhhh, calm down, Dani," my dad said soothingly. "I just wanted—"

"But he's twenty-seven," I interrupted. I had started crying without even realizing it. "He's only twenty-seven, daddy. How could he die? He's only twenty-seven." I repeated it like a mantra.

"I know, Dani," my dad's voice had gotten higher, and I could tell he was trying hard to stay composed.

"What happened?" I finally asked.

"We don't really know yet," he admitted. "They think it was a brain aneurism."

I closed my eyes. Fred. He and his brother, Joey, were childhood friends of mine and my brother. Our parents had known one another since almost before we were all born. We had gone on family vacations together, done family dinners…they were literally an extension of our family. I could not believe Fred was gone. I hung up with my dad and faced some curious faces in my office. I gave them the *Reader's Digest* version and went to go splash cold water on my face in the bathroom. *This must be what shock feels like*, I realized. It felt like I was moving underwater and everything was in slow motion. Back in my office I could not focus on anything, so I emailed Matt: *Can u meet me downstairs for a minute?* He wrote back right away, *Sure, see u in 5.*

I waited for him near the small candy/stationary store on the first floor. I was lost in thought, staring in the other direction, when he came up behind me.

"Boo," he said smiling. Then he saw my face, and his smile faded. "What's wrong?" he asked in alarm.

"I just talked to my dad, and he told me that Fred passed away this morning." I felt my face start to crumple, and I started breathing in and out to keep calm. "He's twenty-seven, and now he's dead!" I felt hysterics rising up inside me and turned to start walking.

Matt fell in step beside me. "I can't believe this! This is terrible. I am so, so sorry." He grabbed my arm and made me stop walking.

I looked at him teary-eyed. "I just don't get it, you know?" I choked. "He was such a good person. It's just not fair."

Matt raised his shoulders. "Stuff like this is never fair," he said gently, brushing tears off my face. "It's tragic and it's terrible and there's no way to understand it."

I nodded and drew a shuddering breath. "I know, you're right. You just never think this kind of thing will happen to someone you know." I shook my head, still unable to accept the weight of the news.

"C'mon, I'll walk you back to the elevator," he said soothingly. "Why don't you leave work now? You're not going to get anything more done today anyway. There's no way your boss will make you stay."

"Okay," I agreed tiredly. As we walked back to the elevator, I saw Christina stepping off and looking around. She spotted us and leaned against the wall to wait. I turned to Matt. "Thank you," I said seriously. "I really needed to see you."

He squeezed my shoulders. "That's what I'm here for," he waved at Christina and headed to his own elevator bank.

"Hey, Chris," I smiled wanly, "thanks for coming to check on me."

"Don't even mention it." She pressed the button to call the elevator. "You ready to go back up? Maybe you should call it a day and head home to your family?"

"Yeah, Matt suggested that too. I think it's a good idea." We went upstairs, and I gathered up my things and headed home. I lay on the couch and tried to watch TV. Then I paced around the house for hours. Matt called to check on me. I told him I was staying home with my family and would call him in the morning. The hours rolled by slowly, and with my parents acting like zombies and my brother opting to go out, by eleven o'clock I had serious cabin fever. I decided to get dressed and go over to the bar Matt was at to distract myself.

At the bar, I was just as miserable as I was at home. He bounced all over the bar, talking to all sorts of people who I did not know, not introducing them to me, and getting completely trashed. I stayed near the bar talking to a couple of his friends who I did know, and coincidentally, one of my own friends ended up being there as well. Two girls seemed to be trying to monopolize Matt all night with heavy conversation. He was always extricating himself from them and glancing at me. His friend Mike was leaning on the bar next to me and also noticed.

"They are friends with his ex-girlfriend." He took a swallow from his beer. "They are probably giving him shit for being here with you."

"*Is* he here with me?" I asked sarcastically. "I've barely talked to him all night. Of all days for him to act like a jerk...." I shook my head. I could not believe how adolescent he was behaving. I came out because I thought he would cheer me up, but he was all over the place acting like a jackass. *It's time to leave*, I realized. *Coming here had been a mistake.*

"Hey, Matt!" He was talking to some people I had never seen before, and I tapped him hard from behind. He spun around and looked almost surprised that it was me. "Okay, you seem really busy," I said coldly, "so I'm just going to leave, okay? Happy Thanksgiving." I turned and started to make my way through the crowd before he even responded.

He caught up with me at the door. "Don't leave! Why are you leaving?" He was completely drunk. I wondered how he even planned to get home from the bar.

"I'm leaving because I came here to see you, yet right now is the first time I've talked to you all night. So have a good time with your friends, or whoever these people are. I'll talk to you later." I quickly walked out of the bar, disappointed that he had been so selfish on a day when I really needed him the most.

"I'm coming with you!" I heard him call out from behind me. I turned around. He was hurrying to catch up to me. "I'm sorry," he said breathlessly when he caught up. "I thought you'd be home with your family tonight, and I drank way too much, so by the time you got here, I just...I am...I'm sorry," he finally got out. "Let's go home. I've been a jerk. Please, let's just go home, and say you forgive me?"

It was cold, and I was tired. The last thing I wanted to do was fight with him, so I relented. "Okay," I agreed. "Let's go home."

I lay in his bed with him for hours, unable to sleep but needing to feel him next to me—needing our connection so badly, I could not bring myself to leave. Finally I dragged myself out his door at six in the morning and drove home, dreading what the next few days would hold.

My dad had picked up my grandma for her to spend Thanksgiving at our house, as usual, but I could barely spend any time with her between going over to Fred's parents' house for support on Thanksgiving and trying to find out the wake and funeral service details for the days following. Thanksgiving night, I finally had a chance to call Matt back. He had left me two messages earlier in the day.

"Hey you," I said when he picked up. "How was your Turkey Day? I am exhausted."

"I bet," he said sympathetically. "Mine was good, nothing out of the ordinary."

I could hear faint music in the background. "Are you in your car?" I asked.

"Oh yeah, I'm heading over to my buddy's place in White Plains. Needed a break from all the family, you know?"

"Well not really," I admitted. "I kind of really want to be around mine right now. But normally, yes, I know what you mean. Is he having a party tonight or something?"

"Not exactly," Matt said slowly. "A bunch of us guys are going over tonight, and then we're all heading to Atlantic City tomorrow. Someone got a comped room," he added quickly.

I was speechless for second, completely caught off guard. "You're going to Atlantic City for the whole weekend?" I finally asked incredulously.

"No, not the whole weekend," he defended. "I'll be back late Saturday night."

I could not even come up with a response. It was unbelievable to me that he was taking off for a fun-filled weekend with the boys when I was going through hell. I had not even planned to ask him to attend the wake or the funeral, but I had counted on him being around afterwards for support. I felt wounded. "I have to go," I announced suddenly. "Talk to you later."

"Daniell—" he started to say, but I hung up the phone.

The wake the next day was pure misery. The whole tragedy just hit me so much harder seeing Fred lying in a casket, painted like a porcelain doll. While staring at him, my father eventually had to nudge me along to shake me out of my grief-stricken stupor. When I arrived home, my friend Melissa, who was up for the holiday weekend, had gathered together Elise and my friends Natali and Sharon for a liquor and cookie binge at my parents' house. Spending the next few hours with them made me feel slightly more human. At about midnight, as they were all filing out the door, Melissa hesitated and stopped.

"I tried to get in touch with Matt," she started, "because I thought he should be here, but he didn't return my message, and I guess I'm just wondering...why *isn't* he here?"

I swallowed hard. "He went to Atlantic City with some of his friends this weekend." I looked at her face to gauge her reaction.

She looked confused, then horrified. "You mean he doesn't know yet? Oh God, my message is going to be terrible when he gets it!"

"No, no it's fine," I insisted. "He knows already."

"Wait, he knew, and he still went to Atlantic City? Would he have been out money if he canceled the room?"

I shook my head. "His friend had a comped room," I said miserably.

Melissa now looked pissed. "You mean to tell me that someone you grew up with *died* two days ago, and Matt decided to gallivant with his friends in AC instead of sticking around for you?" She shook her head. "I'm sorry, Dani, that is just plain selfish and...and fucked up! Who does that? That's a terrible thing to do to you! I hope you make him grovel when he comes back!" She shook her head again and kissed me on the cheek. "Goodnight, and good luck at the funeral tomorrow. Call me if you need me."

I nodded wordlessly and stood at the door while she drove away. Melissa had unearthed what I had been pushing to the furthest recesses of my mind since the day Fred passed. Matt had found it so easy to desert me when I really needed him. What did that say about him? Or about our relationship? I would never do something like that to him. I put my head in my hands. It was all too much; I could only deal with one heartache at a time. And right now, mourning Fred was all I could handle.

seven

DEATH TO THOSE WHO PEE
IN THE MIDDLE URINAL

"Character is much easier kept than recovered." —*Thomas Paine*

I was at my parents' house watching television one night when Merck's commercial for the HPV vaccine came on the screen.

"I want to be one less!" an attractive young girl announced, smiling. "Tell someone today about HPV so *they* can be one less too!"

I laughed to myself about how it was not that long ago that I could not mention HPV without getting a blank stare, and now there was a nationwide campaign from a leading pharmaceutical company. Go figure.

"What's HPV?" My mom had walked into the room and was catching the end of the commercial, where the female doctor was explaining the new vaccine Gardasil. "That's not what you had, is it? I heard them say sexually transmitted!"

Christ. I rolled my eyes. I knew this day would come. "They did *not* say sexually transmitted. And yes, HPV is what I had. Three out of four women contract it, so if I *hadn't* gotten it, I would practically be a medical marvel." I flipped to a different channel and glanced at her, hoping that this would end the conversation. Her eyes had narrowed. My mom could drive me crazier than most people, but stupid she was not.

"What do you mean three out of four?" she asked. "That's ridiculous! Is this a new thing?"

"No, ma," I sighed, "it's the virus that can cause cervical cancer. They have a vaccine for it now, which I'm going to get soon—the first one, anyway."

"Cancer? This thing causes cancer?"

"No!" I said exasperated. "Maybe! Not…always. You shouldn't worry about it. I don't have it anymore, so why stress over it."

"Well what you do mean you're getting the *first one*? How many shots is it?" she asked suspiciously.

"It's three."

"Why is it three?"

"Mom!"

"What? I'm just asking! You don't tell me anything, and now you say that all those visits to Dr. Bernstein were for this thing that causes cancer. Excuse me, *may* cause cancer," she added when I opened my mouth, "and I think I'm entitled to ask a few questions, Danielle!" She looked worried, and I tried not to sound as frustrated as I felt.

"I don't have cancer, I'm not *going* to have cancer, *I am fine.*" I turned back to the TV to signify that the discussion was closed. She walked in front of me to block my view of the television. Reluctantly I looked up at her.

She was staring hard at me. "Do you still like boys?" she asked bluntly.

I nearly choked. "What? First I have cancer, now I'm a lesbian?" I could not help it; I just lost it completely. Laughed until I was practically crying. Laughed until no sound was coming out and my stomach hurt.

She stood there with an embarrassed but determined face. "Well do you?" she persisted.

"No," I shook my head and got up off the couch, recognizing that it was long past time to head back to my apartment. "I'm a huge lesbian now. *Huge.* I listen to k.d. lang, don't shave, and I'm moving in with Jane and Kara, my two lesbian friends." I grabbed my bag and car keys and headed out the door.

"That's not funny, Dani!" my mom shouted after me.

* * *

Going for my first Gardasil shot was slightly nerve-wracking. Definitely not as bad as when I had the cryosurgery or the LEEP, but a vaccine that was hot off the FDA approval list made me a tiny bit nervous. I typically did not get side effects from anything; hopefully the same was true for this shot.

"Hi, Danielle! How are you doing?" Dr. Choe smiled as she swept into the room. She had become my new OB/GYN since Dr. Bernstein had taken medical leave due to back surgery. She had his personality bottled into a young female body. I barely felt a pinch when she injected the vaccine, comfortably relaxing thereafter. Vaccine shots had always been a cinch for me, but rubella, mumps, and meningitis vaccines did not hold a candle to the importance of this one. "Make sure you rotate your shoulder a little bit today," she warned as she applied a bandage, "otherwise the area will get kind of sore. Call us if you have any sort of strange reaction, but you should be fine. See you in a month for the next one!" She smiled at me and I smiled back.

One down, two to go. The second one would be in a month, and the third one would be three months after that. The brochure they gave me said that it would protect against four strains of HPV, including the strain that causes genital warts. I shuddered. My one saving grace had been that I did not contract that strain. I think if I had gotten genital warts from sleeping with one person, I would have hung it up for good. No more sex—ever. I wonder if there is some sort of discount if you buy a lifetime supply of batteries for a vibrator?

Four months after that first shot, I left my gynecologist's office feeling that same surge of relief I felt the day I finally had a normal pap smear. It was officially over. And I felt amazingly free. Enough time had passed since I had last seen Matt that I had started to feel like myself again—on most days, anyway. I could still get down occasionally, but overall I was not lying in bed every morning, dreading to face the day, like I had done earlier in the year. The year continued to pass quickly, but still I had no interest in the dating scene; the horrible episode with Kyle had left a bad taste in my mouth, leaving me unwilling to try again with anyone, until…until…I did not really know when…but I knew I was not up for it all just yet.

Even though I had not gotten comfortable with the possibility of a new relationship, I had become far more comfortable discussing HPV with my friends. It was probably because I was no longer facing endless doctor's appointments, or maybe because

Merck had broken the ice with the general public, but either way, it did not embarrass me anymore to talk with any of my friends about it. Some of them seemed a little weirded out by my openness, some were extremely curious, and to my surprise, some ended up admitting that they too had been diagnosed. Probably the biggest bombshell was when I was introduced to a chatty girl named Sandy at a holiday party. She was so open and friendly, I found myself talking to her and her husband for the duration of the party. At one point she excused herself to go to the bathroom and dragged me with her in order to abide by the "girls always go in groups to the bathroom" rule. I was looking in the mirror and reapplying my lipstick, and she was sitting on the toilet when she let out a moan.

"What's the matter?" I asked, slightly uncomfortable and not wanting to glance over at her.

"I just got my period," she announced. "Shit! I was supposed to go to the gyno on Monday too! Now I'm going to have to cancel. And I really shouldn't cancel."

"Why can't you cancel?" I asked, careful to keep my eyes trained on the mirror. "Were you and Scott trying to get pregnant or something? Wouldn't you not have to go anyway because you got your period?"

"No, I have HPV," she said matter-of-factly.

My hand stopped in midair with my lipstick. "You have what?"

"HPV. It's a virus that—"

"I know what HPV is," I interrupted.

"Oh good! Most people get all freaked out and think I have syphilis or something. But I mean, almost everybody has it, so I don't see what the big deal is." She stood up and pulled her skirt back down, flushed the toilet, and came to the sink to wash her hands.

I finally turned to face her. "It doesn't bother you? What about the cryosurgery or the LEEP? That didn't bother you?" I was just blown away by her casual attitude.

"No, I didn't have to have that stuff. I mean, I might one day, but for now they are just tracking it because it's mild and I'm married already, so I guess I just don't care that much. I just wish I didn't have to cancel my appointment; it makes Scott feel better when I get my updates from the doc. Those 'one less' commercials freak him out." She smiled at me. "Ready to go back to the party? Wait a minute…how do you know about the LEEP and the cryo-whatever?"

"Ummm…." I had just met this girl. Could I be as open? It was not really my style. I paused, undecided. "Well…I have it too, I mean *had* it. I don't anymore," I admitted.

"No shit! See, I knew we had a lot in common!" She laughed and I smiled faintly. "C'mon, let's go get a drink." She unlocked the door and strode into the hallway, and I dazedly followed. Who knew that you could bond over an STD?

Not long after the night I met Sandy, my friends Kristin and John announced that they were going to have a baby. Having bought the baby a really cute outfit, I stopped by the house to wish them congratulations in person. Kristin had a slightly poochy stomach; she was four months along and had not totally popped yet. I could not stop staring at her belly, wondering if I would have any trouble when I got married and wanted to have a baby.

"I bet you live at the gynecologist," I commented, thinking how ironic it was that I had felt that way not so long ago.

"You don't even know," she groaned, leaning back on the couch. "I am *always* making an appointment for one thing or another. And I feel like they monitor my weight gain every other day; it's my biggest nightmare realized." We both laughed. "Plus I need to have even more checkups and sonograms than most people," she added, sobering a bit.

I felt my stomach twist sickly. "Why, are they worried about something?"

"No, no," she reassured me quickly, "the baby is fine. It's just that several years ago I had a…procedure…and because of it, if my uterus stretches too much with the baby, well, my cervix… oh never mind, you probably don't need to hear any of that," she shook her head dismissively.

I could not believe my ears. She *had* to have had a LEEP. That *had* to be the procedure to which she was referring. "Just a random guess," I said cautiously, "but was the procedure called a LEEP?"

"Yes!" How did you know? She looked completely shocked.

"Wild guess," I said wryly. "I've had one too. You really had one years ago? And the only problem you're having is extra sonograms?"

"Yup," she was nodding. "That's all. Why?"

I let out a huge breath. She did not seem at all perturbed, just like Sandy. "I don't know…." I felt my chest tighten a little, remembering how terrified I had been when I was first diagnosed. "Before the LEEP, my doctor said that he preferred to not do it on women before they had children because it could interfere with carrying a pregnancy full term…I don't know," I repeated. "So I guess it's been in the back of my head ever since, scaring the crap out of me."

"Well I'm living proof that all you'll have to deal with is more doctor appointments," she reassured me. "And really, it could be worse, so I shouldn't even complain."

I nodded my silent agreement. I left Kristin's that day feeling more than a little relieved. It felt like a lifetime ago that I believed no one had ever heard of HPV, having felt so isolated by my diagnosis. *Sex and the City* was one of my favorite shows, and all four of them slept around with every new guy they met. Miranda got chlamydia, and Samantha had an HIV test, but by and large they had faced no real consequences. In college, girls scoffed and laughed when I admitted to being a virgin. For a long time I really believed all these people around me were sleeping around with whomever they pleased but were somehow able to bypass all the vaginal torture I had been put through at the doctor's office. Having met Sandy—and now with Kristin safely being in her second trimester—my whole perspective had changed. If there were three of us with different situations pertaining to HPV, there had to be thousands more who wondered if anyone understood what they were facing. Obviously most girls were not going to be like Sandy—offering their diagnosis at a social event—but there had to be more women who felt the way I did. In my case, I at least knew who had passed the disease to me. I could point a finger without any doubts. But I was a rare case. I wondered about all the women who had more-active sex lives and who probably had no idea who had given them HPV. That had to be even more frustrating, I realized.

* * *

"Don't forget my egg rolls!" Jane yelled to Kara. Kara looked at me and rolled her eyes. She was on the phone ordering Chinese food for the three of us. The two of them lived down in Highland Park, and I had driven down to spend a lazy Friday night with them, consisting of Chinese takeout, movies, and girl talk. Kara finished giving the order and hung up the phone. We stretched out on the two couches in the living room and flipped on the TV.

"So what's going on with you guys?" I asked, taking a sip of the wine Kara had just poured.

"Ehh, not much," Jane replied distractedly, flipping through the channels.

"I'm looking into forming my own LLC so I'll have my own photography business," Kara offered.

"Kara, that's awesome!" I was thrilled. I was probably biased as her friend, but Kara was an extremely talented photographer, yet she worked in a bank to pay the bills. Her gift would not go unnoticed for too long, my experience with her being the perfect example. I had always hated my profile, yet she repeatedly told me that it was great and that I just needed to let her photograph me to prove it. Reluctantly I let her do it one day and was amazed at the results. My profile looked better than Christy Turlington. Her hands and her camera possess some kind of magic, because any other time I have taken pictures in profile, my nose always looks huge and crooked.

"Well, we'll see," she said cautiously. "I also want to go back to school." Kara's main goal was to be a forensic photographer and take pictures of crime scenes.

"What's going on with you, Dani?" Jane smiled at me. "How's work?"

"Work is okay," I said unenthusiastically. The truth was that I was burnt out on recruiting but had no idea what kind of career change I would want to make. More than anything, I needed to get away from the poisonous vice president of our company. I had spent my life accepting that women would always be competitive and sometimes spiteful, but when a man is? Pathetic and lame— yet dangerous if he was in a position where his opinion could be taken seriously rather than written off as the petty jealousy I knew it to be.

"How about those shots you were getting?" Jane asked. "Did you get them all?"

"Yup! All three," I confirmed with a grin. "Now I'm totally healthy again."

"I should get the shots," Kara announced.

I looked at her in surprise.

"Even gay people can get it, Dani," she said sardonically, noting my look. "In fact, I was diagnosed with it a few years back, but I no longer have it. I probably got it from one of the stupid boyfriends I had before I came out."

"I don't have it," Jane declared proudly. "But my sister had it. She's fine though. She's actually pregnant with her third kid right now."

"Seriously?" I was in shock. "Your sister has had two kids? Did she have any problems because of the HPV? Did she have a LEEP or cryosurgery?" The questions would not stop spilling out of my mouth.

"Oh yeah!" Jane waved her hand dismissively. "My sister had all the stuff you did, and she is perfectly fine. No problems with the first two, and the third one is coming along great."

"Well I didn't have that stuff," Kara wrinkled her nose, "but I had that horrible biopsy. That was the worst thing I have ever been through in my life."

"Oh my God, I know!" I agreed. "The biopsy was awful, especially because medical students were observing that day so every little thing was being explained. I wanted to die! But the cryosurgery was bad too. And then leaking water for ten days? Terrible. Don't even get me started on the LEEP. You haven't lived until you see your bloody insides on a medical tray and then throw up on yourself."

Jane and Kara let out a collective *ewwww*, and then we all laughed. I could not believe I was actually finding humor in things that had caused me so much misery such a short time ago. I suddenly recalled a class with my social studies teacher in middle school when he was describing the television show *M*A*S*H*, which was not designed for my generation.

"War is miserable business," he had said, pacing at the front of the room. "War is tragedy and death, and if you fall too deep into the horror of it, sometimes you can't readjust to normal life afterwards. *M*A*S*H* took place during a war, but it had comic relief, almost to give people hope that no matter how awful the situation is, you find a way to laugh at nonsense and keep yourself sane."

I had never really appreciated *M*A*S*H*, but I always remembered what my teacher had said about it. The notion of keeping yourself sane, even in what feels like the seventh circle of hell, had struck a chord with me then and had now become somewhat of a proverb.

"What about boys, Dani?" Jane demanded. "I need some juicy news!"

I shrugged. "Sorry, nothing to report." I felt my face turn a little red. I do not know why, but people always expected me to have some exciting dating story because I was single. A good portion of the time I could give them a funny bad date story, but lately I had nothing. Nada. Zip. Zero. Zilch. It was kind of embarrassing. After all, I was pretty darn cute, but I just was not having any luck meeting someone. Almost a year had passed since the unfortunate incident with Kyle, but I had barely even had a crush in that time. I might have even been revirginized.

"You need a boyfriend," Jane said decisively, "and not a putz like the last one. A good one, with a good job and money, so you can marry him."

"She doesn't *need* a boyfriend or a husband," Kara informed Jane. "Dani is taking her time, and she's allowed to be picky. Leave her alone."

"I'm just saying—" Jane started to protest.

"And I'm disagreeing," Kara interrupted.

I laughed as they faced off from opposite couches. "How about we talk about when *you* two are getting married," I suggested.

"It will be in the Bahamas," Kara answered immediately.

I looked at Jane and raised my eyebrows.

"Whatever my baby wants, my baby gets," she announced.

"Well I'm totally down to go to the Bahamas for your wedding." I raised my wine glass in a mock toast. The doorbell rang then, and Jane ran to get her wallet while Kara went to let the Chinese delivery guy inside. I twirled my almost-empty wine glass and felt a slight pang. When *would* I find a boyfriend again? I knew we had just been joking around, and Kara was actually right: I did not *need* one. But seeing the two of them together, as well as Elise and Jack and all my other coupled-up friends sometimes made me wish I could find someone who would accept me, idiosyncrasies and all. Someone who would somehow see me inside the wall I had erected since Matt broke my heart, know that I was in there, and realize that I was worth a little patience and time.

A few weeks later my friend Joe alerted us that there was going to be a bar crawl on the Upper West Side on an upcoming Saturday. A whole group of us went on these crawls a couple of times a year. They always benefited City Harvest, and each person donated two cans of food to pay for a reduced ticket to participate. I had never been on the one that followed a route of bars on the Upper West Side and was really looking forward to trying some new places. Our typical routine was to catch a bus in and back home so no one would have to worry about driving.

That day, we all met up at the first bar, where you are presented with your cup to carry around all day. The place was called Jake's Dilemma. Bar crawls always sort of pass in a blur for me. They start slow and then, all of a sudden, a couple of hours have passed, everyone is tipsy, and it just feels like St. Patrick's Day, without the ridiculous congestion of people. And every single person is not dressed in green.

We were in our third bar on the crawl when I met Brad. I had noticed him when I first walked into the bar and had pointed him out to Elise.

"He's cute!" she approved. "And tall," she added.

"One more beer and I'll go talk to him," I decided aloud.

"Do it," she nodded.

I never had to worry about Elise encouraging me to talk to strange boys when we were out. She was always all about it. Before going to refill our beers, I decided to go to the bathroom. On my way back, I could see this guy and his group of friends; they were making a toast, and he grabbed my arm as I was passing.

"Hey, come hang out," he invited.

God, he's even cuter up close. "Okay," I agreed quickly.

He pulled my arm into their circle of outraised hands. "Happy birthday!" they all yelled.

"Happy birthday!" I shouted a second afterwards. They all laughed and started to chug their beers. I stood there stupidly with my empty cup for a minute, but then Brad noticed and poured half of his into mine.

"There you go," he smiled. "Now drink up, and we'll go get a refill."

"Okay!" I smiled back.

"You are adorable," he said suddenly. "And your eyes are amazing; I noticed them the second you walked in here. I'm Brad, by the way."

"Thanks, Brad. I'm Danielle." I fidgeted nervously. He was pretty direct, but I kind of liked his confidence. I drank from my cup to hide my face in case I was turning red. Elise wandered over then.

"I've been looking for you! You went to the bathroom like eight years ago, I—" she noticed that I was standing next to the guy I had pointed out earlier and stopped talking.

"Hey, Elise," I said loudly, "this is Brad. Brad, this is Elise, my best friend." They shook hands, and we all talked for a minute or two, then Elise discreetly excused herself, squeezing my arm as she left.

"So another beer?" Brad turned to me and dangled his empty cup. His friends had wandered over to the pool tables in the back, but periodically I caught them staring over to check their friend's progress.

"Yes, let's go get one." I followed him to the bar and leaned against it. The alcohol was starting to hit me pretty hard. We stayed near the bar talking. We had about three more beers, just standing there trading information about ourselves, when one of his friends came over.

"Yo, Brad, we're leaving," he said bluntly, looking at me somewhat apologetically.

"I don't want to," Brad replied just as bluntly.

I smiled to myself. Matt would have never said that.

His friend looked uncomfortable. "C'mon, dude, I get it, but it's Mark's birthday, and he wants to leave, so I mean, we have to go." He started backing away towards the door. "Let's go, Brad," he said finally.

Brad and I stood there in silence for a minute. I wondered what I should do. *Ask him to stay? On the other hand, he really should go for his friend's birthday*, I thought disappointedly.

"Let me get your number," Brad was pulling out his phone.

"Um, ok, it's 2-0-1…." I recited my number for him and pulled out my own phone to get his.

"Let's go, Brad!" two guys shouted from outside the bar door.

"Shit! I'm coming!" he yelled back. "Look, I'll just call you in two seconds, and then you'll have my phone number. Let's meet up later at one of the other bars maybe? I'll call you," he promised. Disappointment must have been apparent on my face.

"What's wrong?" he asked, searching my face.

"Nothing! I just wish you could stay. But it's your friend's birthday, so you should go," I smiled. "It's cool, just call me later, and like you said, maybe we'll meet up at one of the other bars."

"Okay, I'll talk to you later." He turned to leave and then stopped. He turned around and looked at me funny.

I raised my eyebrows. "Yes? Did you forget something?" I teased. He looked indecisive, and then, before I knew what was happening, he strode over and kissed me in front of the entire bar.

"Yeah, Dani!" I could hear Elise cheering, and I smiled in the midst of kissing him.

"Okay then." Brad straightened up, and I stood there flushed. "*Now* I'll go. I better see you later," he warned with a smile and then ran out to the door to catch up with his impatient friends.

I headed over to where Elise was waiting with some of our other friends. "Dani has a crush," Elise announced as I got closer. "Look at her, she's glowing. That guy was cuuuute!"

"That guy was an asshole," Joe announced.

Surprised, I looked at him and noticed some of the other guys were nodding in agreement.

"What do you mean he's an asshole?" Elise demanded. "You didn't even talk to him!"

"Doesn't matter. He's an asshole," Joe reaffirmed. "When I was in the bathroom before, he came and used the middle urinal."

Elise and I looked at each other and completely cracked up. "*That* is what you're basing this on?" I sputtered "He's an asshole because he used the middle urinal? That makes *no* sense! You're crazy."

"I'm serious, Dani," Joe insisted. "Ask anyone. No one uses the middle urinal when the end ones are available. It just isn't done."

"Well, if anything, I would think that would make you assume he's gay, not an asshole," Elise reasoned. "But this whole thing is stupid. He's not an asshole or gay, and Dani likes him, so whatever."

"Yes, and Dani has *such* good taste in guys; we should just trust her," Joe cracked. "Her track record for sniffing out assholes doesn't stand up too well."

I felt like the wind had been knocked out of me. Beer tears

began to rise up, but I knew I did not want to lose it in the middle of a bar crawl, so I fought them back. Still, my face must have looked stricken.

"Dani? Dani? Are you okay? I didn't mean it like that..." Joe sounded apologetic.

I shook my head. I did not want to hear anymore. I started to back away and looked at Elise. She looked alarmed, so my face must have looked terrible. I turned and ran out of the bar and up the block as if I hoped running would calm me down. It was dark by now. I stopped at a parking meter and leaned on it, almost hugging it. I could not believe how rattled I was, but what Joe had said hit a little too close to home. I did not have a great track record—but hearing a good friend remark on it with such disdain made me feel pathetic.

"Dani?" Elise had come up behind me. "Are you all right? Joe is just drunk. He doesn't know what he's talking about! Don't worry. I think this guy Brad seems really nice."

"It's not just that," I whispered. Tears were sliding out now, fast and furious. I kept my back to Elise while I wrestled with a decision. We stood there silently for a few minutes, and then I finally turned around to face her. "I mean, he's right," I choked out. "Look at me! My track record is horrendous! And Matt...I mean how can you be so wrong? I was *so* wrong! He was nothing like what I believed him to be—not even close—and it took me so long to see it. How do you get over that?" I asked her tearfully. "How do you try again when you failed so badly the last time around? I wouldn't trust my judgment either." I leaned on the parking meter for support. Now it was time for the hard part. "I also lied to you for a long time."

Elise had looked ready to refute everything I was saying, but now she looked confused. "What do you mean you lied?" she asked slowly.

"Remember when I told you that I was completely done with Matt?" I looked at her, and she nodded. "Well I lied," my voice came out high-pitched as I tried to control it from breaking. "I kept seeing him for a long time after that. And I felt *terrible*, and it *was* terrible, but I couldn't stop myself, and I couldn't tell you because I knew it was wrong and bad, but I couldn't, I couldn't...." I was crying hard now. Elise stood there motionless. I could not bear to look at her. I had always thought I would keep this secret from her, but too many beers were now releasing my shameful secret in torrents. "I'm so sorry," I whispered, once I got myself under control.

"Whoa," Elise said. "I knew that it went on a little while longer. I mean, I'm not stupid, but I didn't know it went on...for how long?"

"Almost another year," I admitted, finally looking up at her.

"Holy shit," she looked stunned. "That I did not know."

We stood there in silence again. It had gotten cooler outside, and I was shivering.

"Dani." She said my name as if she were not sure what she was going to say next. Another long moment passed. "Dani...I don't want you to ever feel like you can't tell me something—ever. You can always, always, always tell me anything. It doesn't matter what it is. Okay? And so you were with the wrong guy. Big deal! You know how many people end up with the wrong person at some point? At least you didn't marry him. At least you did finally see him for the selfish person he really was, and you did something about it. He's going to remember you for the rest of his life as the girl he lost because he was too dumb to figure out how to keep you. You're going to find someone who isn't going to let you down like he did, okay?"

"Okay," I agreed quietly. We looked at each other for a minute, and then she reached out to hug me. We hugged for a long time. I noticed that she did not say she forgave me, and I did not blame her. Nobody likes a liar.

Later that night, Brad called to say what bar he was at, but I was already on my way home, exhausted from my purge of emotions and secrets.

"Oh no, you're already going home?" he sounded disappointed, and even in my exhausted state, I felt a surge of something: excitement, interest…perhaps satisfaction? Something good—that was for sure.

"Call me tomorrow," I suggested. "We can make plans to hang out during the week because next weekend I have a business trip to Florida."

"Well I definitely have to see you before then!" he asserted.

I smiled. "Okay, then I'll talk to you tomorrow?"

"Count on it!" he said. "Have a good night, Danielle."

"Goodnight, Brad."

I spent the next couple of days playing phone tag with Brad, to the point of extreme frustration. If I left my phone for even one second, that was the very second he would call. On the third day, my phone rang really late at night, and I scrambled to answer it, but was half asleep and did not get to it in time. I cursed as I tried to focus my eyes on the phone and see if the missed call was from Brad. It wasn't. It was a number not attached to a name or a contact. "What the…" I muttered. Then a cold wave of shock hit me. It was Matt's number. I had deleted him as a contact months and months earlier, but his number still rang a bell in my brain. I squinted at the clock. Three thirty in the morning. *What the hell is he doing calling me at three thirty in the morning when I haven't seen him or spoken to him in over a year?* My voicemail tone beeped, and I dialed in to listen. It was nothing. Just light breathing, a sigh, and then a click. *Unbelievable.* But typical Matt. My phone started to ring again, and I snatched it, angry now and ready to have it out.

"Dani? It's Mom. Grandma's sick."

I leaned back on the pillows, feeling ill. It had to be bad for my mom to be up and calling so late. "What's wrong?" I asked numbly.

"Well, we don't know," my mom spoke carefully. "She hasn't been feeling so well for a little while, and tonight she went into the hospital. I'll get the room number, and you can call her tomorrow. Talking to you will cheer her up."

Mentally I flashed back to when my grandfather had his heart attack and went into the hospital. I was six years old and had drawn a picture for my mom to give him since, according to hospital policy, I was too young to be allowed up to his room. "This is great!" she had said. "This will definitely cheer him up and make him feel better!" My grandfather had passed away a few days later without me having a chance to see him.

After I hung up with my mom, I tossed and turned all night. My grandma had been in the hospital numerous times in my life and had always been fine. I punched my pillow and tried to relax. She was a tough lady and had beaten colon cancer and leukemia. She would be fine. She had to be.

COME BACK TO BED

"Wisdom is knowing what to do next; virtue is doing it."
—*David Starr Jordan*

"It's not that I *don't* love you. Because in case you haven't noticed, it's all I do! The problem is bigger. I can't…love you enough for the both of us. I don't know how else to put it. This all just feels so one-sided to me. I can't keep giving…when you're not giving back." I waited for a response, wondering how he would react, but Matt sat there silently. I had no idea if he was even looking at me; I kept my gaze trained on the pattern of the blanket on his bed—it was the only thing that was keeping me from crying and becoming a sniveling mess. We had just made love for what I believed would be the last time, and almost immediately after, I had blurted out that our relationship was over. I honestly did not see how he could be at all surprised by the news.

After taking off for Atlantic City when Fred passed away, he had the audacity to desert me again the prior night. New Year's Eve, a night when we should have been together making resolutions for a wonderful new year *together* and kissing at midnight, he actually made other plans excluding me. I flushed angrily thinking about how humiliating it had been to be at Jack's party, awkwardly explaining why I had arrived alone. I made circles on the bed with my finger, trying to take a breath so my voice would not crack. "You keep hurting me. You say that you don't mean to or you'll make it up to me, but you just keep doing it. I mean, I'm clearly not even a consideration in anything that you do!" I could hear my voice getting more and more high-pitched. "Do you want to be with someone else? Were you with someone else last night?" My voice broke on the last word. I did not even want to know. I was so battered. If the answer was yes…. *Please let it be no*, I prayed. The tears started to fall then, and I turned into his pillow and cried like the world was collapsing. And for me, it was. I had come over knowing that I was going to officially end it. It had not even been a choice.

"No! No, there's no other girl! You know that," he whispered urgently as he put his arms around me. "I'm sorry, I know I screwed up last night and when Fred died, but I swear it's not going to happen again."

I could not turn and look at him. I felt like my entire body was splintering into a thousand pieces. My fingertips ached.

"I think," I said haltingly and through tears, "that I need to walk away from you. I can't keep letting you hurt me, and I know you will if I stay. It just has to be easier to not see you at all than it is to feel like this. Even when I'm happy, I won't really be happy. I'll just be waiting for the day when you hurt me all over again."

With that, I pulled out of his arms and slowly started putting on my clothes.

He grabbed me, pulled me back down to his chest, and turned me to face him. "You're not leaving," he looked at me intently and a little fearfully. "You can't. I love you, and I'm sorry. I know I don't say it enough, but I really love you—more than anything. You know that. You know *me*." He was talking so quickly, I stopped crying in amazement. He started nodding his head, almost to himself. "We're going to work this out. Just please don't leave. I can't let you leave, okay?"

I started to open my mouth to refute what he was saying, but he leaned in and kissed me—passionately. Took my hands and held them down over my head as he kissed me so I could not fight back. When he finally let me up for air, I could only stare at him. My heart felt like a weight in my chest. I was hurt and exhausted, and I could not even find words to argue with him.

"I've told you before, and it's true…I've never met anyone like you," he said quietly. "You make me feel things that I'm not used to! I want you more than I've ever wanted anybody and…I…I just don't know anyone at all like you."

I felt the anger start to seep in again. "Just saying that isn't enough anymore! That all means nothing after what you've done! Why do you keep hurting me? You *know* that you're doing it! I don't understand. How can I believe anything you say when *everything* you do contradicts it? This is so hard for me, I mean, *ridiculously* hard, and you are just coasting along for…for…I don't even know!" I snatched my socks from the end of the bed and put them on, then started looking for my boots. He tried to grab me and pull me back again, but I was ready for it and slipped off the bed so he could not reach. I knelt down to zip up my boots, then stood up, looking down on him and feeling slightly superior that I was dressed and he was not. He looked helpless and pained, and I felt my anger start to slip away; the crushing sadness was sneaking back in to replace it. *Can I do this?* I thought despairingly. *Never talk to him, or laugh with him...or worse, never let him hold me, kiss me, stay up late whispering in the dark?* My resolve was slipping, and the weight in my chest had settled into a sharp pain that was spreading everywhere in my body. I felt my eyes welling up again, grabbed my bag and coat, and ran to the door of his room, hoping to get away before he could say anything else that could potentially convince me to stay.

Through the blur of my tears, I attempted to pull the knob twice, before I realized the door was locked. I could hear him put his sweatpants on and come up behind me. I closed my eyes, wishing I could just lean against him, that it was all just a silly argument that could easily be settled. This is what had pulled us together in the first place: this undeniable, overpowering physical chemistry that never seemed to fizzle, even after unforgivable relationship sins were committed. He gently touched my shoulders and turned me to face him. I stared at his chest, unwilling to look him in the eye. I was still crying. He hugged me tight and started kissing my face, my forehead, my cheeks...everywhere except my mouth. Finally I tipped my head up, my resolve completely gone now, and gave him access to it. We kissed for a long time. I stood there feeling devastated, exhilarated, and so full of love for him. It hurt like hell, but it all crashed over me with such intensity, I could not bear for it to end. It was like the first time we kissed, but instead of the promise of the unknown, it was signifying the death of "us." The death of my naïveté, I guess, as well as my belief that he was "the one."

I could feel his tears along with my own on my face, and my heart beat painfully in my chest, wondering why he had let us come to this awful moment. Or had I? Did I want too much from him? Were we both equally to blame? Eventually, I put my hand on his chest to create space and stepped back. I unlocked his bedroom door and quickly made my way to the front door before I could weaken again. When I got to my car, I hesitated before opening the door. Looking back, I could see his silhouette in the doorway. As I got in and started the car, out of the corner of my eye I saw him step forward into the porch light. Against the will of my heart, I put the car into drive, quickly pulled away from the house, and headed down the street. In the rearview mirror, I watched him watch me drive away.

I drove home, crying so hysterically at points that I needed to pull over because I could not even see two feet in front of me through the blur of tears. My phone went off about twenty times. Text messages, phone calls. All him. When I got home, I wearily climbed into my bed and lay there, too tired to think but too exhausted to sleep. I looked at all his text messages. *I'm sorry* was the most prominent. *I love you* was another. The last one said, *Please let me know when u get home.* I pressed reply to that one and wrote, *Home in bed goodnight.* Not ten seconds later my phone buzzed. I looked at it. *Wish I was with u. I know I ruined everything. I'm sorry. Wish I could do it all over differently.* The sharp pain in my chest had turned back into a dull, heavy weight. I rolled over and slowly drifted into an uneasy sleep.

* * *

"So…how did it go with Matt?" Elise was looking at me sympathetically.

We were sitting at Dunkin' Donuts—the one we used to hang out at PDA (pre-drinking age). I felt my eyes start to tear up, and I busied myself with taking a sip of my tea. Just the mention of his name caused a huge lump in my throat. I took another sip of tea and grimaced. Who drinks tea at Dunkin' Donuts? My stomach had been so queasy since I woke up that morning, I could not even handle hot chocolate, let alone coffee. Matt had called three times, and each time I had watched it go into voicemail, the chunks rising in my throat. This breakup seemed dead set on wreaking havoc on my entire body.

"It was…hard." I stared at the table, feeling my eyes well up yet again, yet too tired to fight it. I looked up at Elise and attempted a smile as the tears spilled over onto my cheeks. I felt my face crumple, but I fiercely sucked in a breath and then another until the urge to break into hysterics passed again.

Elise reached across the table and touched my hand. "I'm so sorry, Dani," she said simply. "I can't even say that I know what you're going through…" she shook her head. "I wish I could make you feel better."

I nodded wordlessly and squeezed her hand. "He told me he loved me and that he was sorry." I paused and had to breathe again. "But I told him that it just wasn't enou—" My voice had turned into a squeak as I tried not to cry, and I cut myself off. The nausea I had felt all day rose in my throat again. "I can't eat…I haven't eaten all day. I don't want to eat." I looked at Elise helplessly. "I never thought that people break up when they love each other. I just don't get it…I mean…for me it was so easy. I loved him and wanted to be with him. End of story." I put my head in my hands and whispered, "Is there something wrong with me?

Was I not enough?"

"No! No, Dani! Absolutely not! There's something wrong with him that he took someone like you for granted. You're gorgeous and smart, and you did everything for him—more than you probably should have," she added with a knowing look.

I peeked at her between the gaps in my fingers. She never liked Matt. And when he pulled his disappearing act last month during the memorial services for Fred, her opinion of him had dropped even lower, if that was possible. So did mine once my haze of grief had lessened slightly a few weeks later. I just could not admit it and face being alone. But then, New Year's Eve was the last bit of a looong fuse before I finally blew.

* * *

"Soooo, are you excited?" I squeezed Matt's hand. It was December 29, and we were walking out to the parking lot at our office building. It was possible that we were the only two people who did not have any vacation days left to use that week except for what was built into our office calendars; the parking lot was vacant.

"About what?" he struggled to get his gloves on.

I rolled my eyes. "Um…what else? New Year's!" I danced ahead of him. The last month had been rocky, but I had never been with someone for New Year's, especially not someone I cared about so much. And even though I had always found New Year's to be vastly overrated, I found it kind of thrilling to finally have someone I loved to kiss at midnight this year. He looked amused while I skipped around and circled him.

"New Year's is overrated," he said.

I stopped skipping. "Well duh, everyone knows that. But *you* get to kiss *me* when the ball drops—*that* is what you should be excited about," I informed him, smiling.

"Oh, right." He laughed and fidgeted with the sleeves of his coat. "But aren't you going to Elise's boyfriend's house?"

"*We*," I corrected. "*We* are going to Jack's house. You need to meet him and stop calling him 'Elise's boyfriend.'" I dug my car keys out of my pocket so I would not have to fumble in the cold at my car.

"I actually made other plans," Matt announced awkwardly.

I spun around to face him. "You did what?" I cried. Then I relaxed. "That's not funny. Don't mess with me, you punk."

"No, I really did," he was looking over my head. "One of the people I work with is having a small, low-key house party. I said I would go."

I stared at him, still waiting for him to say it was a joke. "I don't get it," I said dumbly.

He was still fidgeting. "Well I figured that you were going to Elise's boyfriend's house, so I—"

"His name is Jack," I shouted, cutting him off, "and you'd know that if you bothered to get to know *any* of my friends. I can't believe you're doing this to me. After everything that's happened in the last month, I can't *believe* you." I started running to my car, needing to get away before I cried or just decked him in the face.

He kept calling my phone after I ran away from him and drove off. I finally answered around eleven o'clock at night. "What do you want?" I asked rudely.

"I just want to explain," he said helplessly.

"Explain what? Why you don't want to be with me on New Year's Eve? Or how about the fact that you're choosing to go hang out with coworkers over me—coworkers whom you constantly say you can't *stand*. Or maybe you want to tell me about why you disappeared when Fred died?"

Matt was silent. "I didn't disappear," he said hesitantly. "I saw you the night before Thanksgiving, the same day he died."

I pressed a hand to my forehead and closed my eyes, remembering that night. "You've got to be kidding me. That's not a night to bring up in your defense." I shook my head in disbelief.

"And anyway," he rushed to defend himself further, "this whole month you haven't been yourself. I'm just trying to give you some space."

"I haven't been myself? Okay, well I don't know how I'm supposed to act when my friend whom I've known practically since birth dies! Maybe you can find the Hallmark card for such an occasion, huh, Matt? The last thing I *need* from you is space. The last thing I *want* from you is *space*." I was getting slightly hysterical. We had never had a serious argument before this, but all my anger and sadness from the past month was spilling out all at once. "I was dying inside," I said, my voice cracking, "and you were nowhere to be found for two whole days."

"I called you though! I told you that the guys and I were going to Atlantic City. I figured you had enough family and friends around, you didn't need me…" he trailed off uncertainly.

"You didn't want me to need you," I burst out angrily, "because that's what was convenient for *you*. All I needed was for you to be there when I got home from the wake, the funeral…. You just didn't want to be there for me. Your little trip to Atlantic City got you out of having to deal with anything. I guess what they say is true: it takes a real catastrophe to really see what people are made of…."

"What the hell is that supposed to mean?" he demanded.

"What do you *think* it means," I retorted. "I suffered a…a… tragedy, and look how you reacted! You ran as fast as you could in the opposite direction. It's a true testament to your character." We sat there, both of us not speaking for a few minutes. "Just go," I finally said. "Go to your stupid work party with the people you *supposedly* don't even like. And I'll remember that your priorities never include me." I already knew that I had to break up with him. I just was not able to bring myself to say the actual words that night. But the unspoken implication was there hanging between us…just waiting.

At Jack's party, about half the guests knew that Matt and I were on shaky ground, and with their sympathetic smiles, would ask me if I was all right. The other half asked me all night where my boyfriend was and told me how much they wanted to meet him. To combat my discomfort over the whole situation, I downed five green apple martinis and a few shots, and played several games of beer pong. I was discovered passed out in the upstairs bedroom shortly after midnight. My goal of drinking until I felt absolutely nothing had clearly been achieved. I woke up sometime later to someone poking me. It was Jack's friend Greg. He had a girlfriend, but that did not usually prevent him from spitting game at anything with a vagina. I fought to open my eyes all the way, but a stabbing pain in my forehead prevented me. *Ugh, I have a hangover already.*

"What do you want, Greg?" I tried to say, but my mouth felt like it was full of sand, and it was all garbled.

"I just came to say goodnight. We're leaving." He came around the side of the bed and leaned down to hug me. I carefully turned my face away and hugged him. He held on for way longer than what I deemed appropriate.

"Okay...okay...*okay!*" I wriggled out of his grasp. "Goodnight, Greg, I'm sure Alison is waiting for you." I rolled over, but I could feel him standing there at the foot of the bed, just staring at me. *What a stupid fuck. All guys are dicks*, I thought morosely. Eventually, he sighed deeply and walked out. As I was drifting back to sleep, I had another pang of sadness. *Maybe Matt is trying to get in bed with some girl at his coworker's party...and maybe she is not saying no*, I thought bitterly. I fell asleep, tormented by images of him clinking champagne glasses and kissing beautiful girls when the clock turned to midnight.

I drove straight to Piermont the next morning, my head still throbbing from all the alcohol. I pulled into my usual parking spot, facing the Tappan Zee Bridge and Hudson River. This had always been my place. I wrote in my journal here, ran along the pier, walked my dog, and just sat in the gazebo and watched the world. Just sitting here could give me a sense of peace and calm. That morning I just felt numb. I needed closure with Matt—an official end. I would have to go see him today and tell him that I refused to be in this sham of a relationship any longer. Tears burned the back of my eyelids as I stared through the windshield, wondering why he made something that should have been so easy so damn difficult. I loved him to distraction and actually entertained thoughts of marriage and growing old together. Until him, I could never even picture myself married before I was at least thirty. He had changed my mind. I felt disillusioned, sad, and tired.

My phone beeped, and I flipped it open to see a text message from Matt. It read, *I'm sorry to bother you...did you get my message?* I closed the phone and looked at the front screen. There was a little envelope in the right hand corner. Hope erupted inside me, but then I squashed it. Some drunken message from last night did not erase what he had done. What was the point of going one place if all he was going to do was call me and leave a message saying he wished he was with me instead? So stupid! What the *hell* was wrong with him? Angrily, I flipped open the phone and dialed into my voicemail. I punched in my password so violently, I messed up twice and had to start over. "You have…one…new… voice…message," the electronic Verizon siren announced. I closed my eyes and slunk down in my seat.

"Hey…it's me…it's a little after midnight," he coughed uncomfortably. "I just wanted to say I'm sorry…and I miss you… and, umm, Happy New Year, okay? I hope you're having a really good time at Elise's boyf— I mean Jack's party. See, I remembered his name," he laughed nervously. "So I guess you probably hate me, but…I had to call…okay, that's it. Happy New Year again… okay…bye." He sighed before he actually ended the call.

I opened my eyes and stared bleakly out the windshield, across the Hudson River. For a couple of minutes, I counted the cars going by on the bridge. I closed my eyes again. There was a pounding in my head and ringing in my ears. The ringing was getting louder. And it had a melody. Reminiscent of a nineties hit song. *Shit, my phone is ringing.* I looked at the caller ID. It was Matt. *Shit. Should I answer?*

"Hello." I wanted to say something snarky and biting, but my mind was blank.

"Hi." He sounded uncomfortable.

"Why are you calling me?" I was too sad and tired to even sound annoyed.

"Well I wanted to make sure you got my message…" he

trailed off uncertainly, "and maybe see if you wanted to come over later? I could give you a belated New Year's kiss!" he added with a nervous laugh.

I buried my head in my steering wheel, trying to block out his stupidity. "So it's okay to see me the day *after* New Year's," I said dully. "Nobody else you know will be doing anything, so might as well make plans with me."

"What do you mean? I just want to see you. Is that so bad? I want you to know how much I missed you last night...and make it up to you," he hinted meaningfully.

God he was thick, as my grandma would say. "Fine," I agreed dejectedly. "I'll come over later after dinner." In the midst of my misery, I had a small flash of satisfaction in letting him think he was going to get laid, before I kicked his ignorant, inconsiderate ass to the curb.

* * *

At least that had been my plan, I thought guiltily, looking up at Elise and reliving the previous night's events in my mind. But I had been weak and succumbed to our physical connection. He had kissed me the minute I set foot in his house and dragged me to his room before I even had a fighting chance. *At least I had not left there without setting him straight*, I reminded myself, as a fresh wave of hurt washed over me at the memory.

"You need to go out," Elise announced suddenly. "You're hot and single. You're going to meet a ton of new guys—ones who won't hurt you and can't wait to actually *be* with you, rather than just saying they 'miss you soooo much' but never doing anything about it."

I nodded, trying to smile.

"We're going out drinking in the city next weekend," she looked at me hard as if she knew she might have to coerce me, "okay?"

"Okay," I agreed. I could see that alcohol to the point of oblivion might become a pattern at this rate.

The following weekend found us, along with a bunch of our other friends, at The Saloon in New York City—the very same place I threw my birthday celebration the previous year, the night that Matt did not show up. *I should have seen then that he had a tendency to be completely unreliable*, I thought unhappily, nursing a bottle of Miller Lite, wishing to be home in my bed away from the noise and the crowd.

"Hi, I'm Brian."

I pulled myself back from the planet of bitter ex-girlfriends to focus on who had just said hello to me. "Hi…Brian?" I managed to get out.

"Yeah, it's Brian," he smiled.

He had a really adorable smile, I noticed unemotionally. Any other day I would be thrilled that this guy was talking to me.

"Darren told me that I had to get you to come dance with us. So…will you?"

"Darren?" I repeated stupidly. I glanced over Brian's head and could see Elise and Darren standing together in excited anticipation, watching us. *Christ. Really guys?* I knew Darren from college. He was a nice guy, usually a smart guy, but he obviously was a little slow on the uptake tonight, since I was definitely not looking for a setup with a random guy. "How do you know Darren?" I asked finally. *Please let him not say that they just met tonight. If he randomly grabbed a guy and forced him to come talk to me to cheer me up, I'm going to have a conniption.*

"I work with him," Brian said smoothly as he guided me away from the wall on which I had practically planted roots and steered me towards the dance floor.

"Oh," I felt stupid.

Brian was starting to move closer and grind on me in time to the music. Halfheartedly, I put my limp hands on his shoulders and went along with it. I tried to remember if Matt and I had ever danced together. *Oh wait, we did once. The same night that he took my virginity*, I thought miserably. I peeked over to where Elise and Darren had been standing. They were still there, Darren with a big smile and a thumbs-up gesture, Elise mouthing, "Will you please *smile?*" I obliged and pasted a huge fake one on my face. She shook her head and this time mouthed, "He is *cute!*" I nodded and turned my attention back to Brian. He *was* cute…and confident enough to come up to a girl he did not know. I simply could not muster up any enthusiasm. I wanted to, but I felt rigid with this guy's arms around me. The idea of another guy touching me the way Matt did was starting to disgust me the more I thought about it. I then realized I was not moving anymore—and that I might cry on the dance floor in the middle of all these drunk, happy barflies.

"Hey, am I that bad of a dancer?" Brian cracked. He then saw my face. I do not know what it looked like, but judging from his expression, it did not look good. "Are you okay?" he asked, so concerned and sweet that I had to get away from him.

"Bathroom," I stuttered. "I'll be right back." I hurried off the dance floor and went downstairs to the bathroom. I hunched over the sink, breathing deeply and trying to block out the waves of emptiness and sadness. Someone was talking to me in Spanish.

I looked up to see the bathroom attendant trying to hand me a paper towel and motioning for me to move out of the way. After digging in my purse, I pulled out a ten-dollar bill, waved it at her, and stuck it in her basket on the sink. She promptly shut up, and I went back to wallowing in my misery, occasionally splashing water on my overheated face. She then patted my shoulder and handed me a mint.

"Dani, are you all right?" Elise was peeking in the doorway of the bathroom.

"No. I'm not," I admitted. "I just want to go home. Is that okay? I'm sorry. I just can't...yet." I looked at her, pained at what I had turned into tonight. Always without fail I could be the girl who would always have a good time anywhere, no matter what the circumstances. I despised how I felt. Listless. Lethargic. Depressed. Elise did not ask any questions, and we silently went to the coat check to retrieve our jackets.

"Where are you going?" Darren demanded, coming up behind us.

I bristled at his tone. Coming out tonight had been a big deal. I had made it past midnight, which was pretty damn good for how shitty I was feeling.

"Brian thinks you're hot, and you ditched him! Now he's dancing with some other girl up there. You totally blew your chance." He looked at me, clearly peeved, and I wondered why he was being so pushy.

I had been single for about four days. Was I allowed to have a mourning period? Some sort of grieving process? "Sorry, Darren," I said with a phony, bright smile. "Not feeling well. I've got to get out of here. Tell Brian it was nice to meet him." Elise and I hustled out the door before we had to explain ourselves to anyone else who caught us leaving early.

"It'll get better, Dani," Elise reassured me as we shivered on the corner, trying to hail a cab. I burrowed my face into the top of my coat, unable to answer. "The best thing to do—I think," she amended, "is keep going out. It will get easier after awhile. You're going to be okay." I shoved my face further into the warmth of my jacket and prayed that she was right.

A week and a half passed since the night at Matt's house, which I had deemed one of the worst experiences of my life. Each day was slower than the last. I dreaded going to work, opting to arrive really early and leave very late so as to avoid bumping into Matt. After a couple of days of avoiding the gym, I forced myself to go back. But I would sprint into the cardio room, work out, and then hurry back to the locker room. I completely steered clear of the weight room. Occasionally I would allow myself a glimpse and would see him staring at me, watching me rush out the door. My heart broke just a little bit more on those days. One day, as I was rushing to leave, he sidestepped me to get to the men's locker room. Forced to stop running and fall in step behind him, I stared at the floor and silently cursed to myself as he seemed to be deliberately mincing his steps to walk as slowly as possible. Suddenly he stopped, and I almost crashed right into his back.

"Hi." He had turned around and was looking at me intently.

"Hi," I mumbled, looking up at his face and then returning my gaze to the floor. God I loved him. I wished that he had not turned everything into such a disastrous mess. But he had. And being this close to him had me feeling completely sick.

"You look like you've lost weight," he said, sounding concerned.

His observation skills had obviously sharpened in ten days'

time. I had lost about four or five pounds simply from being too nauseous to eat anything. Every night I barely touched dinner. At lunch I would take a bite of a sandwich and then push it away, incapable of swallowing more than one bite. Breakfast did not even exist. "Haven't felt much like eating," I responded curtly, feeling the sickness start to rise up from my stomach. "I've got to go. Have a good night." I stepped around him, wanting him to stop me. *Stop me and say something better than some banal comment about the unhealthy shrinking of my waistline.* He remained silent, and I continued walking a little bit faster, forcing the disappointment back down inside me along with the nausea.

I walked out to my car wondering how long it would take to again find my balance. Every day I drove to and from work with an emptiness in the pit of my stomach and a sick feeling in my heart. Never ever believe people who tell you that "doing the right thing" will make you feel good. Apparently they are either full of shit or they are always doing the wrong thing but are too stupid to know the difference.

"Danielle, are you awake? Did I wake you up? I'm sorry, I'm so sorry. I'm sorry for everything. I really need to talk to you." Matt's voice, garbled and fast, came at me through my cell phone.

I felt like I was underwater; I could not even remember answering the phone. It had to be the middle of the night. "Mm-mmhmmmm, I'm up…" I murmured, trying to wake up and concentrate. "What's wrong? Why are you calling me?" My brain was totally fuzzy, and I wondered if I was dreaming. *We are not together anymore; this is not allowed*, I thought indignantly, then yawned, my eyes slipping closed again.

"Something terrible happened tonight," he said sharply.

My eyes flew open, suddenly wide awake. "What happened?"

I demanded, feeling panic and dread start to take over my body. All I could think was maybe his military brother was being sent to Iraq, or his father had another stroke, or worse, a heart attack.

"One of my bosses died," he said tersely. "The one who had lung cancer. Remember I told you? She was my favorite one. My big raise wouldn't have happened last year without her," he sighed. "I just can't believe it."

I sat there speechless.

"Are you still there?" he asked finally.

"I'm…here. Just in shock, that's all."

"I know, me too. It's crazy!"

"Look, Matt," I said carefully, "I don't want to be mean, but why did you call me? Just because your boss passed away?"

"Well yeah," he admitted, "but also to tell you again how sorry I am for everything I did. Life is too short. I don't want to argue with you. She was in her early forties, married with a couple kids, and now she's gone. I don't get it. I just had to call you and hear your voice. Is that all right?"

"It's actually not," I surprised myself by saying. "I am sorry for your…loss and everything, but I can't be the person you talk to about this. I can't *be there* for you. I just can't do it." I felt my chest tighten. I loved being the person he turned to so much, I could just explode with satisfaction. But I refused to indulge him. Definitely could not—even if I wanted to.

"Please," he begged, "I need to see you tomorrow. Please, can we talk?"

I closed my eyes, struggling to continue with my casual disinterest in his problems. *People do not change*, my brain shrieked at me. How could he expect me to be his sympathetic shoulder about his boss when he had given me nothing to lean on, nothing to hold onto when Fred passed. Fred…. I felt a rush of sadness. Some days I still could not accept that he was gone. "I knew life was too short about two months ago," I said quietly, ignoring his question.

He sighed. "I know! That's what I'm trying to say," he insisted. "I know how wrong I was to do what I did, and I'm sorry!" He took an audible breath. "I'm going to wait for you after work tomorrow, and we're going to talk. And I'm going to hug you! I need to do that, and I'm not taking no for an answer!" He laughed but cut himself off when he realized I had stayed silent.

"Okay," I agreed finally, "I'll meet you tomorrow. You don't get a hug. All you get is conversation. Five minutes of it."

"I'll take it," he sounded less stressed, almost pleased with himself. It made me wary of my decision.

The next day I found him waiting for me, anxiously pacing back and forth near the escalator. He looked haggard and tense.

"Take a ride with me," he suggested as soon as I walked up to him.

I hesitated. I had not promised a ride in the car. Every single time I was in his car we had fooled around or had sex. I had actually been naked more times in his silver Acura than my own shower.

He grabbed my hand. "Please?"

Wordlessly I nodded. Once his fingers had closed around my wrist, I felt the magnetic draw that I had always felt with him. Silently, we walked outside to his car. Matt turned the car on but instead of putting it into drive, he leaned back and sighed. I looked at his profile. It hurt to look at him.

'This was a bad idea," I said uneasily. "I'm just going to go."

As I started to reach for the door handle, he reached across to stop me. "Please don't..." he pleaded. "Can you please...just sit here with me?"

I couldn't answer. His arm was pressed up against my shoulder and my chest. My breathing felt rapid and shallow. I swallowed and looked at him. "Okay," I said quietly. He relaxed and sat back in his seat, but I could still feel where his arm had just been. My heart was pounding.

"Do I get my hug?" he asked, grinning impishly.

My nerves were shot. I could not take being in such close proximity to him, but I wanted to say no. I shrugged with exaggerated indifference for about a millisecond before his arms came around me with stunning force, pressing my face into his neck. I tried to hold my breath as long as possible and ended up gasping for air. The last thing I wanted to do was breathe in his scent. *If I keep my head slightly turned to the left*, I decided, *I could breathe through my mouth and not smell that familiar cologne.* He was stroking my hair and then massaging my neck with his one hand. The console was digging into my stomach, and I had a flash of painful déjà vu, remembering the kiss we had right before he went to Las Vegas and called me his girlfriend for the first time. What was I doing? Sitting in his car *hugging* him? But my arms refused to let go; I was sinking deeper into the familiarity of letting him hold me. Then I smiled. He was making a big show of sniffing me. Inhaling and exhaling in short bursts all over my neck and hair, almost snorting like a dog. It tickled. I jolted back out of his arms.

"Stop it!" I laughed. "It tickles!"

He grabbed my face and kissed me for all of two seconds and then let go. I sat there, stunned. My mouth tingled. I wanted more. He was watching me, waiting for a reaction. "Move your seat back," I whispered. He seemed confused but obliged. As soon as he did, I launched myself over the console and on top of him. "Hi," I looked down at him, smiling coyly.

"Hi," he looked smug and satisfied—a little too satisfied.

I cradled his face in my hands. "I can't stay away from you. I've been trying! And it's impossible. But I can't be around you if you're going to half-ass everything. I can't kiss you until you swear that you won't hurt me like you did. Swear to me." I looked at him solemnly.

"I swear," he immediately said, just as solemnly. He leaned in to kiss me, but I leaned back.

"I need to come first sometimes," I reminded him. "Don't forget that. I could name five guys off the top of my head who would kill to date me," I added half-jokingly.

He looked away. "Don't you think I know that?" he muttered.

Ohhh, I had finally hit a nerve. I squeezed his shoulders and touched his face, forcing him to look at me. "Well then, honey, you probably shouldn't fuck up again!" I drawled exaggeratedly with a smile.

He smiled back. "I swear that I won't hurt you. I just want to make you happy," he said quietly.

I looked at him for a few seconds, letting the weight of what we had decided sink into both our brains. He was getting a second chance. We were officially back together. Then I let him kiss me like there was no tomorrow. Except in the back of my mind, I was acutely and uneasily aware that there was a tomorrow. And in it, I would have to explain to my friends and family that Matt and I were seeing each other again. And no, I was not crazy—I think.

Tomorrow came...and then the next day. I found that I was unable to bring myself to tell anyone the truth. Both my mom and Elise were rejoicing over the fact that it was over, and I did not have the balls to tell them that I had forgiven what we had deemed unforgivable. Months went by, and slowly Matt distanced himself. Everyday conversations began to gradually taper off. Our sex life diminished from daily to weekly to bi-weekly to almost monthly. The strain of all the lying and sneaking around and avoidance of the fact that Matt just wanted to sleep with me because he could sent me knocking on Dr. Olsen's door. One of the first things she told me was that when you cannot resolve an intangible issue in a relationship concerning someone's nature, getting back together is guaranteed to fail. I believed her and lived for our sessions but did not truly face facts until the Coldplay concert, when I was finally forced into confronting what I had refused to believe.

nine

THERE'S NO SUBSTITUTE FOR TIME

"Grief is the price we pay for love." —*Queen Elizabeth II*

"Grandma?"

"Oh, Dani! How are you doing?"

"I'm good, Grandma. How are *you* doing?" I instilled as much cheer in my voice as I could, but she sounded awful. I had never heard her sound like this. She sounded like she had bronchitis and just could not clear her throat.

"So-so. Better than yesterday," she claimed.

I did not believe her. It was a long-running Sepulveres tradition to play down sickness or illness so as not to worry the family. Obviously I was guilty of carrying on the tradition as well. "Well that's good," I said with false brightness, feeling the pit in my stomach even more than when my mom had called with the news. "So did they say what's wrong?"

"No, not yet," she started to cough just then, and I could hear what sounded like a mountain of phlegm in her throat.

Maybe it is *bronchitis…or pneumonia.*

"What's new with you?" she crackled after her coughing fit.

"Not much really. I'm going to Florida for work in a few days."

"That's nice. Now how's your job?" she asked.

"It's okay," I hedged, not wanting our conversation to turn negative at all. Work was actually starting to border on terrible. "Did I tell you I was coaching softball? Mostly the same girls I coached in soccer last year. They are a lot of fun."

"Oh yeah? That's very nice!" her voice cleared a little, and she started to sound more like herself.

I relaxed a little bit.

"How are they doing?" she asked.

"With me as their coach, they will be better than the New York Mets!" I laughed. She laughed too. Our whole family followed the Mets in good times and bad—mostly bad. Her laughing turned into a cough and then another coughing fit. I cringed. *Maybe she should go rest.* "Grandma," I said loudly, "do you have some water? Maybe you should ring the nurse for some?"

"I have some," she said, her voice full of phlegm again. Now she sounded tired. I could hear people in the background and assumed a doctor or nurse had come into the room, because she said, "Okay, Dani…" which is what she always said when she was ready to get off the phone.

"Okay, Grandma, feel better. I'll call you later," I promised.

"Okay, thank you. Take care of yourself, and I love ya."

"I love you too, Grandma," I said softly and hung up. I believed that she could be tough one more time and get through this. I just did not want to think about the alternative.

A few days later I sat in the airport waiting for my row to be announced. I called my mother to say I was getting ready to board.

"Hey, Dani," she answered. She sounded strange, and immediately my hackles rose.

"What's going on?" I asked cautiously.

"Nothing! Are you on the plane?"

"Not yet. Where are you?" I could hear all this background noise behind her voice.

"In the car." She stopped.

I started to get angry. Something was clearly going on, and she was purposely being vague. "Where. Are. You. Going?" I asked through gritted teeth.

"Oh look, we're passing the airport! Wave to Dani, everybody!" she called out.

"You're passing Newark? Are you going to see Grandma? Is she all right?"

"She is fine," she said firmly. It's a nice day, and we decided to drive down and go visit. Uncle Frank has been there every day, and we wanted to give him a break.

"Are you telling me the truth?" I demanded.

"Yes, Danielle, Grandma is just fine. When you get to Florida, call the hospital and say hello. We'll probably all still be there."

"Okay," I said warily, not totally believing her. Right then, the announcement calling for all rows to board came over the loudspeaker. "Okay, we're boarding, I gotta go," I said hastily.

"Have a safe flight! Call us when you land! Love you!"

"Bye, Mom, love you too." I picked up my bags and headed onto the plane. Once I got settled in my seat, the Xanax I had taken a half hour earlier started to kick in, making me feel much more relaxed. A few minutes later, the plane headed down the runway, and I drifted off to sleep, hoping my mom was being truthful with me. *Hang on, Grandma*, I prayed sleepily. *Just hang on.*

"I'm here!" I squinted. It always seemed ten times sunnier in Florida than anywhere else in the world. After calling and calling to no avail, I once again had redialed my mom's phone and was leaving a message. "I'm here," I repeated, "I don't know where you guys are. No one is answering. I'm getting on the shuttle to my hotel…sooo…call me please!" I hung up and shook my head. This did not bode well for my nerves, especially since my anxiety medication had dissipated. I had forgotten to bring the hospital phone number with me.

"Hello?" I had scrambled to get to the phone; I heard it ringing as I was trying to use the key card to open the door to my room and carry all my bags.

"Dani? How's Florida?" It was my mom.

Finally. I dropped all my bags in a heap near the door and sat down on the bed. "It's good. How's Grandma?"

"She actually wasn't doing so well today. She was in a lot of distress," my mom admitted, "and that's why we went down."

"I knew it! I knew something was wrong!" Why did you do that? I would rather be able to see Grandma than be down here!" I felt helpless and aggravated.

"You had to go for work," my mom reminded me, "and Grandma knows that. She knows you love her and that you'll see her when you get back."

"Okay, but what if, what if…I don't know." Superstitious fears prevented me from saying it out loud. "You said she was in distress. I mean, do they even know what's wrong with her? She thinks she has a bad cold. It's not bronchitis, is it? I know it isn't!"

"No, it's not," my mom said quietly. "They found a tumor on her lung. It's the size of a tennis ball."

I was stunned into silence. I had known it would be cancer, but the actual words still hit hard. "So…what now?" I lay back on the bed and closed my eyes. The last place I wanted to be was Florida. I felt completely out of the loop and adamant that my grandma needed me in that hospital room with her.

"Once Grandma gets a little stronger they will give her treatment."

"You mean chemo," I said dully.

"Yes, chemo," my mom confirmed.

I sighed. It was so unfair. Grandmas were supposed to cook, sit in their rocking chairs, and enjoy their grandchildren—not have to go through chemotherapy for a third time. *She has had enough*, I thought fiercely. *She fought through two cancers, the loss of my grandpa twenty years earlier, and she does not deserve this!* "Have they given a prognosis?" I asked finally.

"Not really," my mom said and sighed. "Today was a bad day, but we'll see what tomorrow is like and talk to the doctors some more."

"Okay. I've got to go get ready now for some welcome cocktail party downstairs. Please call me if anything happens," I warned.

"Okay, have a good time. And remember, Grandma always knows how much you love her."

I closed my eyes again. I wished my mom would stop saying that. Grandma had probably seen the entire family in her hospital room today and wondered why I was not there. I felt so guilty, I could not even swallow. "Bye, Mom." I hung up and rolled over. The last thing I wanted to do was get dressed and go downstairs to schmooze. *Please God*, I prayed. *Please take care of her until I get back.*

The next day and a half dragged, but the news was welcome. My mom called to say that Grandma had shown signs of improvement and that the hospital had talked about sending her over to a rehabilitation facility to gain her strength back before initiating the cancer treatment and allowing her to go home. I flew home, the two-hour flight feeling more like six hours; I was so anxious to get back to New Jersey. Immediately after I landed, my mother and I drove down to the hospital.

I had no concept of what to prepare for once I arrived. *Will there be a lot of tubes? Will she look different?* Timidly I followed my mom into the elevator and off at the third floor. My steps became slower and slower as we approached her room. As my mom walked in first, she turned and put a finger to her lips. I peeked in and saw that Grandma was asleep. I walked into the room and absorbed every detail. She was not in the bed; she was sitting in a chair next to the bed, fast asleep and snoring. I had a quick flash of the days we would show up to her house and find her fast asleep in her armchair in front of the television. Except here, she was connected to tubes at every angle. And she looked old—really old—as if she had aged twenty years since I had last seen her a month earlier at Easter.

"Oh, Grandma," I whispered sadly, my heart in my throat. She looked so fragile. My mom and I sat quietly for a few minutes. "Should we let her sleep?" I asked. "I want her to know I was here, but I don't want to wake her up if she hasn't been sleeping..." I trailed off uncertainly.

My mom walked over and tapped her lightly on the arm, and almost immediately, she opened her eyes and focused on me.

"Dani!" her speech was still garbled like the day we spoke on the phone less than a week ago. "Fran! When did you get here?"

"We've only been here a few minutes," my mom reassured her. "You can go back to sleep if you want. We're just here to keep you company."

My grandma looked back at me. "How was your trip?" she asked.

"It was good," I nodded. My trip had been two days of anxiety and stress; I could barely remember who I spoke to at the conference.

"And how's everything?" She looked at me levelly with her sharp brown eyes, the way she always did. She always wanted the real scoop.

"It's fine," I laughed awkwardly. My heart hurt seeing her like this, and my mind had gone blank of lighthearted topics to discuss. "Want me to turn on the TV?" I offered, reaching for the remote. She made a face, and my hand stilled. She was always amenable to watching something on television. This was out of character.

"If you want, you can turn it on," she said dismissively. "I don't want to watch anything."

I looked at my mom, and she raised her eyebrows. "C'mon, Grandma," she coaxed, "we'll find a good show or movie to watch."

Grandma shrugged as best as she could while hooked in to fifteen machines. I scanned through some channels until I landed on Animal Planet, and we watched silly pet videos for an hour, which she actually ended up enjoying. I caught her smiling more than once as a dog wrestled with the hose or a cat jumped on its owner's head. A short time after that, she began to doze off, so we quickly said our goodbyes and left after she fell back to sleep. The drive home was mostly silent.

"She looks better than she did the day you went to Florida," my mom finally broke into the quiet.

"She doesn't look good though," I rubbed my hand wearily over my eyes.

"She had an oxygen mask that day and couldn't talk. She just squeezed our hands. Today was much better."

I almost swerved off the road as I stared at my mother. I could not believe things had been that bad just a few days earlier. "So you would say things are looking up?" I asked. I could see her shrug out of the corner of my eye.

"Grandma is tough. She's been capable of getting through worse than this, so we'll just pray and hope for the best, okay?"

"Okay," I agreed. What else could we do.

The next few weeks were difficult. Every few days, one of us would make the two-hour drive down to go sit with Grandma in the hospital. My uncle lived closer, so he went as often as possible. My dad drove down every other day, and the rest of us—me, my mom, my brother, my aunt, and my cousins—filled in between. A Saturday was approaching on which I had made plans and reservations months earlier to go to Atlantic City with some friends. But Saturdays were usually when I would go with my parents to the hospital. I decided to make my trip to the hospital on the Thursday prior so I would not have to alter an entire weekend for the group heading to AC. But that Sunday, while checking out of the hotel, no one needed a ride, so as I was driving back alone, I decided I would stop in the hospital for another visit.

"Hi, Grandma."

"Dani! Are you here by yourself?" She struggled to get the words out. Her speech had become more and more incoherent as time had passed, and not one doctor had any explanation for it. Sometimes it was clear as a bell, and sometimes I had to really concentrate to make out what she was saying.

"Yeah, remember I said I was going to Atlantic City? I thought I'd stop by on the way home and see how you were doing." I squeezed her hand and pulled up the chair so I could sit closer to the bed.

"Did you win any money?" she asked.

"No," I laughed. "No money." I squeezed her hand again.

"Oh well," she sighed. "Maybe next time." She squeezed back and yawned.

"Are you tired? You can go to sleep. I'm just going to sit here for a while," I told her.

"Don't leave without telling me," she warned.

"I won't, Grandma," I promised.

She leaned back, satisfied, and her eyelids started to close. I turned on the television and found the movie *Homeward Bound*. In case she woke up, she could watch something sweet and light. There was a stack of magazines on her bed table. Unsure how outdated they might be, I picked one up and started to flip through it. I came to a page with a big picture of Meredith Vieira and settled back to read the article accompanying it. I had only watched *The View* occasionally, but she had caught my attention there, and now I always watched her on *The Today Show* with Matt Lauer. She was the ultimate woman: classy, well spoken, extremely intelligent, and just a little bit sassy. I was completely engrossed in the article about her life until I reached the part where she spoke about losing her mother. Her description of how she watched her mother take her last breath as she held her in her arms struck me, and I glanced at my grandma. She was sleeping peacefully, her chest rising and falling rhythmically. Tears burned the inside of my eyelids as I tried to imagine it: watching someone draw his or her last breath. *Would you ever be able to erase the image from your memory?* Grandma opened her eyes then and looked over at me.

"Oh good, you're still here," she said sleepily.

"You were only sleeping for a few minutes," I told her gently.

"So how is work? When are you getting a raise?" she asked. Classic grandma.

I smiled. "I don't know, hopefully soon?" I offered. "I'm not sure that I want to work there that much longer though."

"Why, because of that one in your office?" My grandma knew that I could not stomach the VP in my office, and she thought he was *despicable*.

I laughed.

"Well he's a good reason to want to leave," I admitted, "but it's not just that. I don't enjoy going anymore. But I don't know what I want to do next."

"So you try something new! And if it doesn't work out, you try something else." She nodded her head. "Something good will come your way."

"You think so?" I asked.

"Yes. You can do anything," she said firmly and coughed.

She looked tired again, so I went back to my magazine and let her drift back off to sleep. This time an hour and a half went by, and I was starting to feel fatigued from being out so late the night before in Atlantic City. I hesitated to wake her, but I knew she would be upset if I failed to do so. Her hand was still clasped in mine from when I took hold of it a few hours earlier. I squeezed it a little, and she slowly opened her eyes.

"Dani?" She looked at me with tired eyes, and I wished I did not have to leave. I absolutely hated the thought of her being alone in the hospital, even if it would only be a few hours before my uncle would drop in again.

"I just wanted to let you know that I've got to get going," I said softly.

"Do you take care of yourself?" she demanded suddenly.

I stepped back. Her voice had been so weak up until now. "What do you mean 'take care of myself?'" I asked, confused.

She squeezed my wrist. "It's important you take care of yourself. If you don't feel right, you go to the doctor. Do you hear me?" She looked at me so sternly.

I was still confused. "Of course, Grandma, I always go to the doctor when something is wrong."

"Nothing is more important than your health." She looked at me to see some sign that I agreed.

"I know, Grandma, don't worry," I leaned in to kiss her face and hug her. Her outburst had unnerved me. It felt like—and my mind rejected it outright—last words someone would say if unsure whether or not she would see the other person again. I hugged her tightly, feeling her frail body, listening to her heart beat in time with my own.

"I love you, Dani," she said right into my ear. "You, Jon-Paul, Nicole, and Paul. I love all of you, and I'm very proud of you."

My chin started to wobble, and I knew if I stayed even one minute longer, I would completely lose it right in front of her. "I love you too, Grandma," I said tightly. "I'll talk to you later." I let go of her and gave her a bright smile as I grabbed my bag and keys. I paused just to remember how she looked. At that moment, she did not appear as she had looked to me for the past few weeks. Right then she looked the way I always wanted to remember her:

strong and capable, and imparting advice to always make my life better. We held each other's gaze for a quiet minute, and somewhere in my head, I knew it was going to be the last time I would see her. I hurried out of the room as the lump in my throat got bigger and my heart began to ache. Once I got to the parking lot, I started to cry and drove the rest of the way home in a haze of tears.

Two days later, the hospital called and said there was a blockage in my grandmother's lower intestine. They gave her a 20 percent chance of surviving the surgery necessary to remove it. My dad and my uncle agonized over what to do, but in the short time that they had to make a decision, the hospital called back and said her blood pressure had dropped too low to perform any surgery. It was just like her, to step in and make the decision for herself. The next morning, my mother and father, along with my aunt and uncle, drove down to be with her. Hooked up to a morphine drip, she passed away as they all sat around her bed. My mom called me on my cell as I was on my way to work to break the news.

"Dani? Grandma's gone. But she wasn't in any pain, and she's with Grandpa again, so we just have to remember all the wonderful times we had with her—"

I stopped listening. Grandma was gone. My little, tough-yet-sweet grandma was gone. I finished the drive into work just to inform them all what had happened and then let Christina accompany me on the drive to my parents' house.

"I'm so sorry, Dani," she said simply. "If there's anything you need, just let me know."

I nodded and blew my nose. It was embarrassing how much of a crybaby I had turned into these past few years. Once I was at my parents' house, I set myself to work. I pulled out all the old photo albums and started extracting pictures for the wake and funeral. Hours went by, and I got lost in the bittersweet task. My phone started to ring. It was Brad. I stared at the phone, somewhat astonished. He had been calling me for weeks, and I had barely made the effort to call him back because I had been so distracted.

"Hello?"

"Oh my God, at least I know you're alive! You have a severe phone tag problem!" he joked.

"Listen, Brad," I started.

"Oh no, am I going to get the just friends speech before we even go out on an official date?" he teased.

I laughed weakly. "No, it's just...I know I didn't say anything...but my grandma has been sick these past few weeks, and today she passed away, so I'm just...I mean I can't—" I fumbled for the right words.

"I am *so* sorry," he breathed. "Now I feel like a total asshole. Seriously, I am really sorry, and I know this is a stupid question, but can I do anything?"

"No, thank you, that's so nice of you, but I'm fine. Well not fine, but you know what I mean. I'm sorry I haven't called you back, it's just been a lot going on over here...."

"Hey, I understand! You have a lot of stuff to deal with right now. I just have one request." He sounded serious now.

"Okay, what's the request?" I asked, tensing.

"That when everything settles down and you feel up to it... you call me, even if it's just to talk," he said soberly.

I relaxed. "I can do that," I promised. "I have to go now though."

"Okay, well again, I'm sorry for your loss, and your family has my condolences," he rushed to add.

"Okay, thank you." I hung up and returned to the task of organizing photos, when my phone rang again.

"Hey, Dani?" It was my mom.

"Yeah, ma, what's up?" I clenched the phone between my shoulder and ear as I flipped through the albums.

"Do you think you can go through the albums for some pictures?" she asked.

"Already doing it," I assured her.

"Also…we want someone from the family to speak at the service. We don't just want some priest who didn't know her like we know her to talk. We want a family member to say something." She paused without actually asking the question.

"I'll do it," I said instantly. It made sense that I would do it. I was the oldest granddaughter, my brother had no interest in public speaking, and my dad or uncle probably would have a hard time with it. I put the albums on hold for a while and went to get a pen and a pad to come up with something that could attempt to honor even a fraction of the person she had been to all of us.

The next few days passed quickly, and before I knew it, I was at the wake. People came and went. Some I knew, some I did not recognize. They all kissed me and told me how wonderful my grandma had been as a friend, a neighbor, an aunt, a sister. There were a lot more people than I expected. Sometime later, my uncle tapped me and said it was time for me to give my speech. Although composed all day, I now shakily made my way to the front of the room.

"Hi, everyone," I said quietly. I cleared my throat. "A year ago I took a writing class where the assignment was to write a character story. We had to pick a real person and describe them in two pages. I chose my grandma because, if anyone was a character, she was, even if she herself didn't know it. Even though I can't even come close to describing her fully in a couple pages, this is what I came up with:

At four foot nothing and barely a hundred pounds, she's still the toughest Sepulveres; no offense, Dad and Uncle Frank. To know her is to love her, even if you are only lucky enough to meet her once. She's opinionated, but she listens, and she's always short and to the point. She always has Kleenex tucked in her watch. She's a great cook, but don't you dare let there be any leftovers. She hates that. But she loves her toothpicks. And you can't ask her in a restaurant if her dish is good; instead of answering, she'll scoop three-quarters of it onto your plate and tell you to try it. But…if you eat three plates of food at her house and are just too full for one more bite, she'll look at you and say, "What's the matter? You don't like it?"

She drinks an extraordinary amount of seltzer and hates when her checkbook is off by three cents. She'll go to an all-you-can-eat buffet and eat a twenty-dollar bowl of soup. She'll stand precariously on tiptoe on a chair to change her clocks, instead of waiting for Donnie or Frankie to do it for her. Sometimes she does more in a week than I do in a month. Movies, beauty parlor, church, shopping…and occasionally she and Grace will even accidentally drive across state lines. She loves sitting in her rocking chair, she loves the color blue, and she loves flowers. She loves looking at pictures of her family and framing the ones we give her, because what she loves most of all is her family. She would do anything for us…unless we needed her to drive us somewhere; it is only then that we're out of luck.

The last time I saw her, I hugged and kissed her goodbye, and she said, 'Dani, I'm so proud of you. You, Jon-Paul, Nicole, and Paul. All of you. And I love you very much.'

A long time ago, Grandma let me have a makeup compact that Grandpa gave her when they were young. There was a note on the box that said 'To My Sweetheart Mary, I send you this token so you know how much I am thinking of you. I miss you and cannot wait to see you. Love Always, Your Sweetheart Paul.' So as much as it hurts us to lose Grandma, at least we know that we're giving her back to Grandpa."

I looked up from my piece of paper and smiled tearfully at everyone in the room. Most smiled back through their own tears, and my uncle walked over and hugged me.

"Thank you, Dani, it was perfect. Just perfect," he repeated, wiping his eyes.

I nodded a thank you and quickly walked away from the front of the room to go hug my dad. I could hear my mom talking to some of the relatives.

"That was her," my mom was saying, nodding emphatically. "That was Grandma in a nutshell." My cousin came over then and hugged me. We stood there hugging for a while, and then more relatives came over to give their condolences. Grace, my grandmother's best friend, slowly made her way over to me.

"We did cross state lines!" she confirmed with a sad smile. "But your grandmother always would say to me, 'I trust you,

Grace! I trust that you will get us home!'" She squeezed my arm. "She was very proud of all of you kids. She talked about all of you all the time."

I leaned down and hugged Grace. She and my grandma had been two peas in a pod; I knew she was going to be lonely without her other half.

The rest of the wake was a blur, and the funeral the next morning went by just as quickly. We had to caravan the funeral procession all the way from Toms River back to Brooklyn, where my grandfather was buried. The priest said a few words, we laid flowers on the casket, and that was it. It was over. If something can feel excruciatingly long and far too short at the same time, it is definitely a funeral. I was exhausted. And I had not even begun to mourn.

We all went to a nearby restaurant for an early dinner that my cousin Joseph had thoughtfully arranged for all of us. I looked around at most of the people at the table. Everyone looked despondent and worn out. It was worse when it was all over, I realized. Knowing that you could never pick up the phone and call the person who was gone. Never see them at another family function or holiday. I really started to feel the depth of the loss and fought against it. It would have to wait until I was home and by myself, so I could embrace all the emotions on my own. Every day I would miss her.

A couple of days later I returned to work, sort of listlessly. Everyone had their sympathetic smiles, and I accepted their condolences. Every morning, the loss of her would hit me all over again. I spent the first couple of weekends sort of holed up in my apartment or at my parents' house, not wanting to see anybody. I was too sad and did not have the energy to pretend otherwise.

After a few weeks of being a hermit, I forced myself to make plans with Elise, and we had a relaxing night just hanging out at her place. I kept feeling the urge to talk about my grandma, and she patiently listened.

"I know that you're supposed to be a little more prepared for losing a grandparent, right?" I asked Elise. "I mean, they're kind of old when you're born, so it's just like a known thing. But this is really hard! She has been around for so many important things, I know, but she's going to miss so many others. Although, I know she's just looking down with my grandpa and wants us all to be happy and do well. It's just hard. I don't know."

"She absolutely wants you to be happy," Elise affirmed. "And of course she's watching. She'll be there when you're just going to work in the morning, and later when you get married, she'll be there too."

I nodded, feeling the lump in my throat grow. Every time I talked about her too much, my heart would ache. "You're right. She wants me to be happy." I agreed. "She always wanted that. Oh, and did I tell you who called the same night that I first found out she was sick?"

"No, who?" she asked.

I made a disgusted face. I could see it dawn on her.

"Are you kidding?" she fumed. "Matt called? Did you answer?"

"It was in the middle of the night, so I didn't even hear it until it was one ring away from going into voicemail. He sort of left a message though." I rolled my eyes.

"A Matt message, right?" Now Elise was making a disgusted face.

"Oh yeah, never normal!" I exclaimed. "He breathed and

then hung up. That was it."

"Are you going to call him back?" I could see her struggle to ask that question, knowing she'd rather say, "You're *not* going to call him, right?"

I shrugged. "Actually I didn't even really remember that he called until today, so I hadn't even thought about it." I watched her open her mouth to say something and then shut it.

"Well if you *do* call him, you'll *tell* me, right?" she inquired pointedly.

"You will be the first to know," I promised.

I drove home that night, wondering how long it would take to get my rhythm back. I felt kind of lost. I thought about what my grandma had said that last day I saw her.

So you try something new and if it doesn't work out, you try something else. You can do anything. I could look for a new job. I could try to find out what it was that I wanted to do with my career. I could take risks. I could take risks…maybe even ones that were not job-related. I pulled out my phone and, after a small pause, dialed a number I was not sure if it was too late to call back.

"Hi, Brad? It's Danielle." I stopped, unsure what to say next.

"Hey, it's good to hear from you!" he exclaimed. "How are you doing? How's your family?"

"We're…surviving," I said, smiling. "Thanks for asking. I know I promised I would give you a call when things got a little quieter, so…" I trailed off not sure if he still wanted to see me; it truly had been awhile since we had first met, and with only sporadic phone interaction since then, he could just be forced into being nice because of my situation.

"So maybe you'd want to hang out?" he finished for me. "How about dinner on Friday? You're still single, right?" he teased. "I'm not going to take you out and hear about your boyfriend troubles, am I?"

"Still single," I confirmed with a laugh. "And available," I added.

acknowledgments

There are so many people to whom I owe a debt of gratitude and thanks for supporting me in my every undertaking. First and foremost is my immediate family: Mom, Dad, J.P., and Maximus. If my mother were not such a character in her own right, the retelling of our conversations in this book would have been ridiculously boring instead of just ridiculous. Thank you to my mom for being wonderful and telling me my entire life to be the bigger person, always turn a deaf ear to gossip and negativity, and pave my own way through life. To my incredible dad, who has graciously accepted that I am uncomfortable with the idea of him reading this book due to the exorbitant mentions of the word *vagina*. To my extremely intelligent brother, J.P., who always thought self-publishing should be my medium instead of waiting for some short-sighted publisher to come to the realization that my writing is brilliant. Good suggestion, bro. And to my little Max, the best dog in the world. He could always be counted on to lick my face and wake me up if I had dozed off across my laptop mid-sentence (or mid-writer's-block). For my extended family, I'm so lucky that you believe in me and all my ideas instead of thinking that I'm a raving, total lunatic. Thank you so much for your love and un-wavering support, Aunt Kathy, Uncle Frank, Nicole, and Paul. Grandma Mary, you are forever in my heart, and I know you're getting a big kick out of all this from where you are.

To my teachers—amazing teachers who encouraged me to continue to write and develop my craft—I appreciate you all so much more than you will ever know. In high school, Mrs. Betsy Panico for refusing to let me drop honors English and Mr. Woody Rudin for nurturing my hidden creative writer underneath my perfectly sculpted, five-paragraph essays. At the University of Delaware, Professor Tom Pauly, who invited me to take part in fascinating research for his book about the life of author Zane Grey, which planted the seed of one day writing a book of my own. And post-college, the fabulous Susan Shapiro, adjunct professor at NYU and author of several top-selling memoirs and novels. Read her books, take her classes; she is a force of nature: susanshapiro.net.

Thank you to Therese Shechter for her blog *The American Virgin* at trixiefilms.com, without which I might have never had the courage to publish a book that broaches the subject of virginity in a world gone sex-crazed. Her blog and documentary film *How To Lose Your Virginity* are equally funny, insightful, and original.

Thank you to the Foundation for Women's Cancer, Patti Murillo-Casa and Tamika Felder of Tamika & Friends (tamikaandfriends.org), Fred Wyand of the American Social Health Association (ASHA), and Lynn White from the Angels of Hope Foundation for being so supportive in promoting my book.

You all work tirelessly to raise awareness and educate women (and men!) to take the initiative to stay healthy and cancer-free. Thank you to everyone at Bergen OB/GYN for taking every measure to keep *me* healthy and cancer-free.

To my amazing friends, I am so lucky to have you in my life. To Jen S. for being the first person to read my manuscript and insist it had to be published. To Jen S., Becky G., Kristi W., Jen G., Cher W., and Kerri T. for keeping me sane when my world was falling apart and for being a part of the best summers that I ever had. To Erica M. for being there from start to finish and then some! To Allison H. for noticing a scrawny, shivering high school freshman and offering me her varsity jacket. To Jackie K. for already suggesting my memoir to her book club. To Eric A. for proving that men and women really can be friends and for providing insight into the male mind when I was at a complete loss to comprehend it. To Greg McGoon for always supporting me every time I have a crazy notion, I'm so happy to have met you in the trenches. To Kat Murello for being talented, brilliant, and wonderful, and for agreeing to do the very first review of my book. Read her amazing blog at ravenouskitten.com. To my "little sis," Michelle L., who is currently trying to figure out how to rent a tractor trailer and dump thousands of copies of my book on Matt Ryan's front lawn. *Hell* to the *no* Michelle, but I love your loyalty! I must also give a shout out to Jodi T. simply because she is one of my favorite people, and she bakes me a delicious cake every year on my birthday. Not only will she tell everyone she knows to buy and read my book, but she will probably bake me a cake in the shape of a book. (I like the raspberry chocolate one Jodi; don't forget.) And to Fred B., you are missed every minute of every day. There is no one in the world with a smile like yours.

Thank you to Bryce Cullen Publishing and David Michael Gettis for making my greatest dream a reality.

And I suppose I finally ought to thank "Matt Ryan" for a great deal of the material contained in this book. As my mother taught me, I will always try to be the bigger person, and I would never wish harm on another person. However...I do believe in karmic retribution, and if it does exist, Matt Ryan has undoubtedly spent the last several years suffering from a chronic case of explosive diarrhea.

about the author

Danielle Sepulveres was born and raised in New Jersey. She attended the University of Delaware and received a BA in mass communication with a minor in English. After several years as a corporate drone in finance and then sales/advertising, she now works in the TV/film industry. Follow her on Twitter: @ellesep

CPSIA information can be obtained at www.ICGtesting.com
Printed in the USA
BVOW05s2010071215

429602BV00002B/29/P